Ryan

C000022368

on the event of your
wedding 26 June '21

every blessing

[signature]

Reflections

Circular emails from a country Vicar under lockdown

By
Kingsley Taylor

Grosvenor House
Publishing Limited

All rights reserved
Copyright © Kingsley Taylor, 2020

The right of Kingsley Taylor to be identified as the author of this
work has been asserted in accordance with Section 78
of the Copyright, Designs and Patents Act 1988

The book cover is copyright to Kingsley Taylor

This book is published by
Grosvenor House Publishing Ltd
Link House
140 The Broadway, Tolworth, Surrey, KT6 7HT.
www.grosvenorhousepublishing.co.uk

This book is sold subject to the conditions that it shall not, by way of
trade or otherwise, be lent, resold, hired out or otherwise circulated
without the author's or publisher's prior consent in any form of binding or
cover other than that in which it is published and
without a similar condition including this condition being imposed
on the subsequent purchaser.

A CIP record for this book
is available from the British Library

ISBN 978-1-83975-297-1

Dedication

To Jo-an who listened to every email I sent with a critical ear and kept me going through the lockdown as I sent them.

Contents

Preface

March 23 2020, the lockdown in response to the Covid-19 Virus in the UK began. People weren't sure what to expect, I suppose everyone was stunned. The Churches were closed and the clergy were not even allowed to enter their churches for prayer.

Recently the three parishes of the Whitland group, Pendine/Velfrey group and Crymych Group were inaugurated as one Local Ministry Area, difficult area to have as a Ministry Area as is spans the three counties of Carmarthenshire, Pembrokeshire and Cardiganshire and stretches from the mountains to the sea. I was appointed LMA Dean, but then the lockdown happened and everything ground to a halt.

I couldn't visit anyone, there were no church services and I couldn't just sit here and do nothing.

I had at least collected emails from someone in each of the fifteen churches so I decided to send a circular email just to let everyone know I was here if needed.

No one knew how long this would last and I had no clear idea what I was going to do next. Perhaps send other emails from time to time. From Palm Sunday

I decided to send a circular every day through Holy Week and such was the response it became a daily circular, every few days more and more people asked to be added to the list and many people sent it on to others as well. I was bowled over and humbled by what people told me it meant to them.

This isn't so much a diary of the lockdown but my rambling musings as I reacted to people's concerns and the events as they developed. These are not mini sermons or thoughts for the day this is just a country Vicar on an inner journey reaching out to others. I have collected them here because I read somewhere that the National Library of Wales thought such things would be useful to future generations in helping them to understand what it was like to live through this. Also because some of the recipients thought they were so good they suggested I put them into a book.

Acknowledgement

Thanks to all the recipients of the emails and especially all who replied with their own stories, their words of encouragement and their thanks.

Part 1 Lockdown

Wed 25 March

Subject: Hello from your friendly LMA Dean

Dear Everyone who I have an email for

Just a quick hello to show that I am still here and to give a little hope in these difficult times.

From a book I am reading - the Celtic Wheel of the Year

Praising

Praise to you who knows our harsh times,

when the universe withdraws its friendliness,

and we are thrown back on our own resources.

For whether we feel your absence or presence

there can be no pretence.

Praise to you who bears our "how long?"

In Stillness

Be still in the silence and aware of the Love with and within......

Opening Out

O Vulnerable One who hears our silent cry,

be with each person this day who is wandering their own lonely desert.

Encircle with your love

those who know there are no short cuts,

who cannot go round but must go through[1]

email if you need anything.

Every blessing

Kingsley

Fri 3 Apr

Subject: Hello again from your friendly LMA dean

Dear All

First of all, I am sending this to all in the Ministry Area who I have emails for, do you know anyone who has an email which I do not know who would like to hear from me?

During this lockdown it is sad that I am not allowed to enter the church. However Wardens are allowed to check on the state of the churches. On Palm Sunday apparently some churchyards are being closed to stop people putting flowers on graves, the advice from the Bishop is basically that it is impossible to stop people

---

[1] Celtic Wheel of the Year by Tess Ward (O books 2007)

doing this, so I suppose as long as people keep their distance I can't see the harm.

With Easter coming up I have been reflecting on the prospect of no Easter services and I have been reading about the practices of the Celtic Church.

In the Celtic Church they used a loaf which they tore apart with great effort which is a better symbol of Christ's torn body than snapping a tidy priest wafer in half and distributing little wafers, everyone had a chunk of bread which they chewed vigorously to get a proper taste. The Chalice was a large bowl and everyone took a good swig not a tiny amount to wet their lips to fully appreciate taking the blood of Jesus into themselves.

Has our celebration of Communion become sanitised? Have we lost sight of the suffering it cost Jesus to give us this memorial? This year, as we cannot celebrate Communion together we can at least reflect on our understanding of what we do when we do celebrate together.

Every blessing

Kingsley

Part 2 Easter

Sun 5 Apr

Subject: Hello from your sad LMA Dean

Dear All

On this Palm Sunday when Jesus triumphantly enters Jerusalem and as we enter holy week I find it sad that we cannot meet together.

I have been reflecting:

FAQ: Where is God in all this?

Glib answer: He is suffering alongside us.

But I do not like glib answers (even when they are right) because they are not the whole answer nor do they meet the needs of the questioner.

Is it an answer to those who are suffering with the virus and those who die (though we trust they are at peace in His Kingdom), is it an answer to the bereaved families who were not allowed to spend the last moments at the bedside to hold a hand and say goodbye, is it an answer to NHS staff who are struggling to cope and who see the suffering and death, is it an answer even to those who have lost jobs and livelihood and face an uncertain future?

I humbly admit I do not have the answer. I can only trust that God has his reasons because the alternative is an uncaring universe where nature quite arbitrarily decided to heal itself.

Another thing I will not do is celebrate when this is over. I will hold a vigil for those who have died.

But today Jesus enters Jerusalem because he has a plan to save us all, and he had to suffer and die to fulfil the plan so whatever the reason for COVID-19 we do have a God who understands.

Every blessing

Kingsley

Mon 6 Apr

Subject: Hello from your reflective LMA Dean

Dear All

The Celtic Church saw the cross as the victory and Jesus as the Victor rather than meekly giving himself up to the shame of the cross. Over and over again in the Bible we are reminded that there is a spiritual warfare and we should arm ourselves with the armour of God. All this week as Jesus is in Jerusalem teaching the people and confronting the religious leaders he is fighting this spiritual battle.

I expect many people have said this COVID-19 is an evil we are fighting or a judgement of God or something,

or one of the last plagues before the end. But things like
this have happened throughout history.

Jesus never once said the Roman invasion was a
judgement on the people of Israel and unlike what his
people expected of the Messiah he did not come to drive
the Romans out. His battle was always spiritual and so
is ours.

It is just poignant that all of us have space this year to
reflect on what Jesus and the cross are to us.

Great and mighty God, conquering hero, as the Easter
weekend approaches, I ask that you reveal to me the
meaning of the cross as a battleground, that I would
pledge my allegiance again to you, my warlord, my
Lord and King, ready to stand for you in the spiritual
battle. Amen.

(Celtic Lent by David Cole)[2]

Regards

Kingsley

Tue 7 Apr

Subject: Hello from your reflective LMA Dean

Dear All

_____

[2] Celtic Lent by David Cole (The Bible Reading Fellowship 2018)

1 We are so used to seeing Jesus depicted as beaten and
2 defeated, falling under the weight of the cross we tend
3 to forget the whole purpose. The Celtic Church saw
4 this more as a spiritual battle and that he had won the
5 spiritual battle in the garden of Gethsemane. He was on
6 his way to defeat the power of evil, to bring us back to
7 God. He may have been weak in body but he was
8 strong in spirit.
9
10 King of the universe, Lord of all things, thank you that
11 you went to the cross for me, but also to save everything
12 from the clasp if sin. Thank you that you approached
13 this knowing the joy set before you, and went with an
14 eager heart, though weak in body. Raise my spirit to
15 step into the trials I face with that same heart. Amen.
16
17 (Celtic Lent by David Cole)
18
19 Kingsley
20
21
22 **Wed 8 Apr**
23 Subject: Hello from your positive LMA Dean
24
25 Dear All
26
27 As you have probably guessed I am reading a book
28 called Celtic Lent by David Cole. Today he talks about
29 our part as warriors in the fight against evil after Jesus
30 has won the battle. Too many churchgoers think it
31 enough just to attend and have their communion. This
32 Easter we cannot attend nor have our communion so
33 how do we define ourselves as Christians? We may all

be separated but as the battle is spiritual rather than 1
physical we can all reassess what it means for each of us 2
to be a Christian and through prayer and discipline we 3
can still fight evil. 4
5
Warlord, as the warriors Joseph and Nicodemus took 6
your body from the cross and laid it in the grave, in that 7
same dedication I give my life to you in the spiritual 8
battle. Under the covering of the protection of your 9
victory and your kingship over all things, call me to 10
arms that I would fight all that wars against your 11
kingdom on this earth. Amen 12
13
(Celtic Lent by David Cole) 14
15
Fight the good fight 16
17
Kingsley 18
19
20

Thu 9 Apr
21
Subject: Hello from your thoughtful LMA Dean 22
23
Dear All 24
25
Today as reflect on Jesus sharing his last supper with his 26
disciples it is hard that we cannot. After supper he took 27
his disciples to the garden where they couldn't keep 28
awake while he struggled in great anguish with his 29
destiny and his human feelings. We each of us after all 30
this time very much isolated from each other may be 31
struggling with our own inner selves. Jesus was arrested 32
and falsely accused, beaten and stripped. And we feel 33

powerless to do anything and are simply existing from day to day.

But Jesus in all he went through was winning the battle for us, how can we not join the battle which for the moment is internal. For all of us this is a wilderness, what is he preparing us for? Be ready when he calls.

Regards

Kingsley

Fri 10 Apr

Subject: Hello from your meditative LMA Dean

Dear All

I am used to doing an hours meditation, but I cannot do an hour on this. Unless I see faces I don't know when you are bored and have simply scrolled to the bottom (like I would).

Jesus died on the cross, he who is life itself was lifeless. The Celts understood his connection with the whole of creation which sometimes we overlook thinking only humanity was affected, yet there was darkness and an earthquake, the creator of all things had died and creation was affected even if humanity so often isn't. He died to free everyone from evil and so many people today would rather cling on to what is wrong. Is there anything in our lives we are hanging on to that we

shouldn't?   In lockdown we have space and time to
reflect, let us not waste it.

To Jesus: Thank you

Kingsley

Sat 11 Apr

Subject: Hello from your waiting LMA Dean

Dear All

Easter Saturday is usually a sort of non-day, an in-
between day. It was a sad day for the disciples because
all they really knew was that Jesus was dead, they had
the promise but we as human beings need to see
something, faith is very hard. The whole of creation
waited, all the angelic host waited, this was something
not even they really knew the outcome of, it was a
totally new experience for them.

We wait, we face something we have never experienced
before, we don't know the outcome as we mechanically
go about our daily routines and nothing seems real.
We can only hang on to hope, God is still in control.
Tomorrow is Easter, the beginning of new life, new
creation. Time marches on and this will end and the
world will be a different place.

Christ who knew death, God who felt the loss of life, as
we ready ourselves for resurrection, show me the power
which this brings. I ask you, Lord, God of the universe,

to release that resurrection power into my life today. Amen.

(Celtic Lent by David Cole)

Kingsley

Sun 12 Apr Easter

Subject: Hello from your celebrating LMA Dean

Dear All

Christ is risen hallelujah

Easter is all about hope, new life, rejoicing. It took a while for this to sink in with the disciples. Also the world around them hadn't changed, they still faced persecution and even death for their faith. But Christ having risen gave them joy and courage to face anything as well as the knowledge that death had also been defeated and the way was open for eternal life.

The world around us has not changed today, we still have a long way to go, but knowing that Christ is risen and defeated the powers of evil can give us hope and the courage to face whatever is ahead, as well as the assurance that all those who have died have the promise of new life too. Jesus does share in our suffering, he has even died for us but Easter reminds us that even suffering and death is not the end.

And finally from Celtic Lent by David Cole

Christ is risen!

He is risen indeed!

Alleluia!

Alleluia!

Let us celebrate and feast and rejoice as the Celtic saints did at the end of Lent. Let the new life of resurrection begin!

Kingsley

1
2
3
4
5
6
7
8
9
10
11
12
13
14
15
16
17
18
19
20
21
22
23
24
25
26
27
28
29
30
31
32
33

Part 3 Long Month

Mon 13 Apr

Subject: Hello again from your friendly LMA Dean

Dear All

Thanks to all who have responded to these, now I have started I can't just stop!

Easter Monday. The disciples are slowly hearing stories of the risen Christ even if they haven't yet met him. Gradually over the next few days more and more of them will have met him and their lives are changed. But he tells them to wait until they have power from on high which will not be until Pentecost.

We are all waiting still, traditionally lent is over but for us it doesn't seem so. We have the advantage of hindsight as far as Jesus disciples are concerned, but not for ourselves. This is still something we must go through day by day. I suspect many of us now know of someone who has COVID-19 and even of someone who has died. But the Easter message is still that of hope and not of fear.

May the blessing of God be upon me,

you who fashioned and formed me.

You love all that you have made

1 and never forget or forsake.

2
Grant me the grace to do justice,
3

4 love kindness and walk humbly with you, my God.

5
(The Celtic Wheel of the Year by Tess Ward)
6

7
Kingsley
8

9

10 **Tue 14 Apr**

11
Subject: LMA daily message
12

13
Dear All
14

15
We have a unique opportunity. Normally we get to
16
Easter and put Lent behind us, we plan events for the
17
summer to get together and raise money, but not this
18
year. The period between Easter and Pentecost for the
19
disciples was a mixture of joy and fear. Jesus would
20
appear when they didn't expect him and continued to
21
teach them and prepare for the task of spreading the
22
gospel, yet there was the ever present risk of arrest and
23
execution. They didn't self-isolate but they kept
24
together as a group away from normal life.
25

26
We have the opportunity now without the business of
27
anything else to draw nearer to God ourselves, to listen
28
to him in our hearts and our private prayers. Pray also
29
for all who die this day.
30

31
May the courage of God go with me
32
33 as I leave the fold of my security.

May the guidance of God be my pilot

When my old map no longer works.

May the love of God keep me

When I feel danger of foe within and without.

And may the Spirit of God lead my heart

All my journey through until I reach the home of heaven.

(The Celtic Wheel of the Year by Tess Ward)

Kingsley

Wed 15 Apr

Subject: LMA circular

Dear All

As the lockdown continues and more and more people are dying, then there is the news that people are dying in care homes that haven't been reported, then there is the harm to the economy and peoples livelihoods, it would be nice to have some good news for a change. Easter is always a message of hope, that Jesus has defeated evil and opened for us the way to eternal life.

But we have to live in the meantime and things are getting hard.

The disciples had to do a lot of waiting at this time while we had the advantage of knowing the outcome, now we are in a time of waiting. We cannot skip a few pages or fast forward, this is something we have to live through. Let us try and learn from this, let us learn patience, compassion and hope. One day we will look back but let us not forget the lessons.

The peace of God which passes all understanding be with you now and always.

Kingsley

Thu 16 Apr

Subject: LMA Round Robin

Dear All

We may feel we are stuck in a loop but remember we are one day closer to the end.

Jesus' disciples by now were probably thinking he would be with them for ever and he would lead them into something, maybe now he would overthrow the authorities and drive the Romans out. But he was preparing them and teaching them for the day he would no longer physically be with them and it would be up to them to spread the good news. The Romans did eventually leave but not for hundreds of years, and where are they today? Even empires come to an end. Yet Christianity is still here, even without the church and the buildings.

On a sad note. Those of you who know V_ will be sad to hear of her passing last night (not COVID-19) but

her health has been failing for a long time. Pray for G_, 1
E_ and H_, the boys will not be able to come to the 2
funeral, it will be G_, me and the undertaker at the 3
graveside. 4
5
6
Bless you all. 7
8
Kingsley 9
10

Fri 17 Apr
11
12
Subject: LMA circular 13
14
Dear All 15
16
During this period there is good and bad, everything is 17
so odd. 18
19
The number of people who die every day is in danger of 20
being a statistic. But every one of them is known by 21
God, they are more than sparrows, and they are loved 22
by families and friends. God will offer to take them and 23
wipe the tears from their eyes and their families will try 24
and give the respect they deserve within the regulations, 25
their souls have the offer of eternal life while those who 26
are left to mourn do their best for the mortal remains 27
that housed for a while that vital soul. 28
29
While nature heals itself and people have found there is 30
a different and better way to live, they do not want to 31
go back to the way things were but hope for a better 32
future. 33

Until the ascension Jesus continues to teach his disciples a different and better way and we as Christians should take this opportunity to look again at the things Jesus said so we can make the world a different and better place even if everyone else forgets.

God be with you all.

Kingsley

Sat 18 Apr

Subject: LMA Saturday

Dear All

From 'The Celtic Wheel of the Year' by Tess Ward

Blessed be you Gone Ahead God,

who went to the nightmare landscape

shutting the doors behind, that we might not have to go.

Protect me as I rise up this day.

Praise to you O Hope bringer.

For even and all the terror we have seen with single eye,

there is no black place without chink or peep or crack,

without seam of escape, or silver vein or glimmer,

because there is no place that you have not visited

with your light of way-through.

Praise to you.

God is here with us, Easter reminds us of his love for us
because Jesus willingly fought evil and defeated it for us
that we may have eternity with him. Kingsley

Sunday 19 Apr

Subject: LMA Easter I

Dear All

In the green book the gospel for today is the road to
Emmaus.   Two people who had heard the stories of
Jesus' resurrection but hadn't really believed.   Then a
stranger comes along wanting to know why they were
so sad and although he explains to them why it had to
happen as it did they still could not recognise him.   Yet
it was in the simple act of breaking bread that the penny
dropped.   They had seen those hands do the same act
before, perhaps at the feeding of the five thousand,
perhaps at many meals they had with him, we don't
know if they were at the last supper.

We are on a journey, a sad journey and we have not
been here before.   Jesus has been travelling with us all
along and perhaps we have not seen.   Look for the little
things, and in them see his hands.

(hand emoji)

Mon 20 Apr

Subject: LMA Week 4 lockdown

Dear All

A survey has found only 9% want things to return to normal after the lockdown, but what is normal? There is the pre COVID-19 normal, there is the lockdown normal which we have at the moment, and there will be the post COVID-19 normal and they are three different things.

Jesus' disciples went through a range of normals. They had their normal lives, then Jesus came and they followed him for three years and that was normal, then his death and resurrection and this became the normal for them at this time when he appeared when unexpected to teach and encourage them, then there will be the period of waiting between his ascension and Pentecost, then the normal of going out in the power of the Spirit to take the good news to the nations.

So, what is normal? There is no such thing.

Live each day as if it special because it is. Experience what is, the sad and the happy, do not dwell on the past or worry about the future, the past is gone and the future is in the hands of God. Take what God gives you today and live.

God's blessings to you all.

Kingsley

Tue 21 Apr

Subject: LMA circular

Dear All

We live in a world of contrast, the sun shines and the
sky is blue and there is so much sadness and fear. We
cope because we have to, but some cope better than
others.

During this after Easter period we think of the disciples
and the uncertainty ahead of them, but they had Jesus
physically among them maybe not all the time but
he was still there and they could see him and talk
to him.

For those who are on their own, those who find it hard
to cope, those who have uncertain futures, those who
have personal tragedy they do not have Jesus physically
with them. It is easy to say he is with you because he
promised, it is easy to quote 'Footprints' but loneliness
and despair is not something you can just brush off.

I just hope that the general care of the communities we
live in can touch those people, even if it is only by
telephone, waving through the window or doing
shopping.

But Jesus is there, even if we can't see him, and God still
loves every one of us.

Kingsley

Wed 22 Apr

Subject: LMA daily

Dear All

Never forget the word cwtch.

I often wonder about the time Jesus spent with his disciples.

In the beginning God enjoyed an evening walk and chat with Adam, until Adam hid from God. Throughout the Old Testament God was continually reaching out to people who so often turned from him.

When Jesus lived a human life he had his parents, brothers and sisters (unless you are a catholic), cousins, friends, disciples. He could be close to other human beings. After the resurrection he could still do this but he knew he would have to leave.

Ever since God has been continually reaching out to people who so often turned from him. By so many ways we put him in isolation sometimes under the guise of religious procedures, when all he wants is to be with us.

Now there is only us, cut off from each other, we have no excuse to let him in.

And when we can let us cwtch again and include God in the cwtch.

A big Virtual Cwtch to you all!

Kingsley

Thu 23 Apr

Subject: LMA continues

Dear All   1
                                                           2
Yesterday I had a zoom meeting with the Bishop,   3
Archdeacon and the other LMA Deans, I'm sure you are   4
all thrilled to know the church is still holding meetings. 5
Be assured that the Church is probably going to let us   6
off some of the ministry share this year, P_ is calling it a 7
year of Jubilee (for those of you who know your Old   8
Testament).   9
                                                          10
I have also been approached about taking a zoom   11
wedding with the legal ceremony to follow next year.   12
                                                          13
                                                          14
Oh, I am having to learn new things. It is good we have   15
this technology but I am not that clever, for instance   16
I still have to type everyone's email in every day.   17
                                                          18
The disciples were learning new things, this was a   19
changing world for them, they were being taught to go   20
out into the world beyond their own people. Jesus   21
promised he would be with them and he would send the   22
Holy Spirit to enable them but it was not the same as   23
having him physically with them.   24
                                                          25
Although we are spirit and we have access direct to God   26
we are still physical and bound to the physical world   27
and can't always feel his presence, and this is because of 28
our shortcomings not his, and do find it hard at times to 29
trust.   30
                                                          31
Technology is a tool, it is useful for us to keep in touch, 32
but it is not the same as meeting together, sharing a coffee. 33

If anyone is interested in having a zoom meeting with me let me know and I will do my best (perhaps on Sundays?).

Every blessing

Kingsley

Fri 24 Apr

Subject: LMA thoughts

Dear All

Last night we decided to go out and clap, it was good to see the neighbours (old and new) even if from a distance.

Have you thought of the first thing you are going to do as soon as you can?

I am going to have a Guinness in Station House! (Oh, shock horror! of all the things the Vicar would want to do first!)

I miss having a coffee with parishioners, I miss having a proper chat. (Oh, Vicar, what about church?)

We have left our comfort zone.

So did Jesus disciples, I wonder if by now it had dawned on them what Jesus was preparing them to do, the call of a disciples is to leave the familiar behind. When we

roll up on church on a Sunday to do our religious bit is
it too comfortable, do we hope God will not speak to us
because he will ask us to leave something and take a
step of faith.

Has he got our full attention now or are we settling into
new comfortable? Can we hear his voice? What is he
asking? What if the churches don't open this year, how
do we express our Christianity?

Thanks to everyone who has responded to these, some
of the responses are very interesting.

Every blessing

Kingsley

Sat 25 Apr

LMA Locked Down

Dear All

For a while it seemed as if time was passing too fast, by
now we would have all planned our summer and the
churches would have all sorts of events lined up. But it
is still only April and it feels like my last email to you
was over a week ago rather than yesterday.

If it wasn't for the sadness and the hardship so many
people are going through which is always at the back of
my mind I would be freer to enjoy this slower pace of
life and the opportunity to reflect and relax.

One of the things I have constantly been reflecting on is how the disciples of Jesus spent this time, it is still a period of intense teaching that they are going through in preparation for the time Jesus will physically leave them. I wonder if the time was fast or slow for them.

I know Jesus is with us all but what we learn from him is down to our ability to hear and the time we are willing to give him to listen. We are so fortunate to live in the country where the glory of nature is all around us and as the Celts understood God is in that nature and can speak to us through it.

'Be still and know that I am God'

Sun 26 Apr

Subject: LMA Easter II

Dear All

The readings in the green book for today are about Jesus the shepherd.

I decided to look again at what I am supposed to do as stated in the Inauguration Service, I was called to share with the Bishop as the chief shepherd in the diocese her ministry in this area with 'gentle oversight and encouragement' and I should exercise ministry with 'gentleness, love and grace'. Lovely words but how can I do that from here?

I go back to the disciples again, they were with the risen 1
Jesus being taught and prepared, they weren't expected 2
to go out until he had ascended and sent the Holy Spirit. 3
                                                          4
Despite my frustration I must take this as a time of 5
preparation. But then it is the commission of all 6
Christian people to spread the good news and perhaps 7
he is preparing us all. Be ready for his call when the 8
time is right.   9
                                                         10
Every Blessing   11
                                                         12
Kingsley   13
                                                         14
                                                         15
Mon 27 Apr
                                                         16
Subject: LMA week 5   17
                                                         18
Dear All   19
                                                         20
After over 1,000 days in lockdown it is still only April. 21
With no weekly structure to our lives it is hard to keep 22
track. Today I wear black and a clerical collar for the 23
first time in millennia but it is not a Sunday so it must 24
be V_'s funeral.   25
                                                         26
I have often wondered about time, we can only measure 27
it by devices that are inside time and Einstein would say 28
it depends where you are and how fast you are going. 29
The first question anyone asks when someone dies is 30
'How old is he/she?'. Does it matter? We are all people 31
loved by God. We are not how many times the earth 32
has circled the sun with us on it. Those who have died 33

of COVID-19, those who have died of other things, those who will die because they have not had the treatment they need, they are all special to God not daily statistics.

While Jesus was on this planet he has friends, he understands our need for human contact, but as God how does he cope? He made us to be with him and from the beginning we have turned our backs. I hope we have all been drawing closer to him at this time.

Kingsley

Tue 28 Apr

Subject: LMA plus

Dear All

I am grateful to those of you who are passing these on to others, but I am also a little humbled that you think they are worth passing on.

I'm sure something Jesus was teaching his disciples was about themselves, who they really were, the people God intended them to be. When I was in college training for the ministry we were studying theology, we were taught ministry, we were given the tools, but we were never taught to face ourselves. I did at one point and it tore my preconceptions apart.

In our previous normal lives when we met with others we all put on a face that we want people to see. In

lockdown we cannot do this, we are compelled to face
ourselves. But we needn't face ourselves alone. God
has made each and every one of us special, that inner
self that is his design is therefore bound to be something
wonderful. We do not have to conform to other people's
ideas but when we truly face ourselves and the person
God designed us to be we can truly be individual.

Every blessing

Kingsley

Wed 29 Apr

Subject: LMA circular

Dear All

In the past I have not thought much about the time
between Easter and the Ascension because there has
been so much going on. I hadn't realised that it was
actually such a long time, Jesus is still with his disciples,
popping in and out of their lives. How much different
his teaching to them was at this time than the pre-Easter
time we will never know because the Bible says very
little about it. Before Easter they were out and about
and he was teaching large gatherings of people and
performing many miracles, now he was only appearing
to his chosen few.

Apart from this circular and a few phone calls I have
no contact with parishioners. I know we are all in the
same situation, we are all in lockdown, so I shouldn't

grumble. So I continue to use it as a time to reflect and
pray and get closer to God, and until it started raining
doing a lot of gardening for Jo-an.

But I also realise how lucky I am to live in the country
where I can see nature in all her glory and in that nature
I can see the working of God's hand. But we all need
to feel God within us, always reaching out to us and
now giving us the space to reach back to him within
ourselves.

The earth rolls on and on through space, the planets
and stars and galaxies continue their dance. Let us open
our hearts to the wonder of God.

Kingsley

Thu 30 Apr

Subject: LMA circular

Dear All

April slowly draws to a close, the longest April on
record, how many of you are getting fidgety and
restless? Yet isn't it better to be fidgety and well.

When Jesus was in the wilderness and he started to get
fidgety the devil came to him promising him an easy
way out and Jesus knew the promises were empty. After
the resurrection and Jesus was back with his disciples,
they probably hoped that it would go on for ever.

Nothing in this world lasts for ever. The hills, mountains, seas, oceans last, they are constant, but even the
world will end. Only God lasts and his promise to us of
everlasting life with him.

Too much of our time we look back at a golden past or
forward to an exciting future. We have no choice but to
live in the moment so don't give up, seek God and learn
whatever he is trying to teach us.

Every blessing

Kingsley

Part 4 New Normal

Fri 1 May

Subject: LMA May 1

Dear All

Finally it is May, I thought it would never come. The earth rolls on through space, the seasons come and go, in time the lockdown will begin to ease and we will be able to catch up.

Jesus is still spending this time teaching his disciples, but don't think it is like they are sitting in rows and he is lecturing them, that was not his way. He used parables, he showed them things around them in a new light, he discussed, we know he had a sense of humour so he probably joked with them too, so they probably had a lot of fun.

I hope we are managing to squeeze in a little fun too.

Look for joy, look for magic, look for the rainbows.

Kingsley

Sat 2 May

Subject: LMA May 2

Dear All

We clap every Thursday for the NHS but there are so many more we should clap for, the farmers, the shop keepers, postmen, delivery drivers, local heroes who shop for those who can't go out, for all the many people who are keeping things going, etc.

We have time to pray, for the dying, for those who suffer, to bereaved families and it is not only through COVID-19, all other illnesses and deaths have not stopped, we pray for a way out of this situation, we pray for a miracle.

Though I have encouraged you to look within and seek God in the quiet we must still remember we are part of the world, of society, and we mustn't become too introverted.

During this period between Easter and the Ascension Jesus was with his disciples, teaching and preparing them, but he was preparing them to go out and take the good news to the world. We also must prepare for our witness as Christians when we can at last go out into the world. Our lives have changed, let us not waste that change.

Kingsley

Sun 3 May

Subject: LMA Sunday Easter III

Dear All

Jesus said 'I am the way, and the truth, and the life;'

How do we define ourselves as Christians without
church? How do we share with one another and Christ
without Communion?

The disciples had been with Jesus up to three years, then
witnessed his death and resurrection and now he is with
them for forty days preparing them. It was hard for
them to come to terms with who he was even so, how
much harder for us who are not physically with him.

Before lockdown out Christian life was simple and
comfortable, we went to church. Now we have to
reassess everything.

I am having to work out how I can be Vicar without
church and without visiting, so if these daily messages
become a bit strange please bear with me.

In all the uncertainty there is only one certainty, 'I am
the way, and the truth, and the life;'

Every blessing

Kingsley

Mon 4 May

Subject: LMA Week 6

Dear All, May the fourth be with you.

We will never know what Jesus taught his disciples or
how he taught them during the period between Easter
and the ascension but one thing we can be sure of is

they didn't have to pass an exam. The people he chose were not rich, powerful, intellectual, etc., they were people like you and me.

We, however, do not have the advantage they had of hearing and seeing directly from him. We have centuries of opinions, disagreements, interpretation, bigotry and preconception to cope with. You go to any bible study and you will find everyone has a different opinion and everyone is right. What is more, everyone has missed the point. The Bible is not a book to be studied and examined minutely, it is a revelation of how to live. Jesus is the ultimate revelation, he did not come to form a committee, he did not come to lecture and found a theological institute, he didn't come even to found the church, he came to live the example of how God wants us to be.

Week 6 of lockdown, have we faced ourselves? Have we worked out what it really means to be a Christian? Have we examined our own preconceptions and biases? These are such strange times and nothing we have learned has prepared us for this. But God is the one constant and he will not change.

Every blessing

Kingsley

Tue 5 May

Subject: LMA round robin

Dear All

Jesus said to his disciples that they were slow to
understand, this is probably part of the reason he spent
so much time with them after the resurrection before he
ascended. So much tradition had to be stripped away
to get to the real truth of what God had been saying
through the Old Testament. Jesus had to criticise the
religious authorities because they put tradition before
the law.

All our tradition has been taken away and I hope it will
not be put back as it was before. But as I said (was it
yesterday?) we all have our biases and preconceptions
and these should be stripped away too.

We have one basic choice, either God or an unfeeling
random universe. Yesterday was what has become Star
Wars day (May the force/fourth be with you) where the
force is the energy of all the people in the universe
binding the universe together, this is probably what a lot
of people who claim to be spiritual believe, but without
God the universe is still unfeeling and random. With
God there is purpose, plan and the promise of eternal life.

If we chose God, he is still there when all else is stripped
away. Today just be with God.

Kingsley

Wed 6 May

Subject: LMA corpulent canary

Dear All

1 What we would all give to be there on the hillside with
2 Jesus disciples and hear his words directly! (Unless we
3 feel safe and comfortable from this distance so we don't
4 really have to commit to anything.) But surely if we open
5 up our hearts and come with no preconceptions, just
6 being prepared to listen, we should be able to hear him.
7
8 I actually believe everything in the Bible is true - which
9 makes me a sort of fundamentalist, rather than those
10 who say we should read it in the context of the time and
11 can therefore pick and choose what we believe in.
12 However, experience (and Jesus himself, and Paul)
13 shows that we cannot judge others for what they believe
14 and write them off as non-Christian simply because
15 they do not believe what we do.
16
17 I had an experience when I was 7 or 8 which has stayed
18 with me and I had to find some way of incorporating it
19 into a Christian theology - which I have, yet there are
20 those who would consider me crazy/deluded/heathen if
21 they knew what it was and how it is still part of my
22 beliefs.
23
24 We each have to find our own way and God will speak
25 to us as individuals if we are open to him. Accept what
26 he says to you. Now is the ideal opportunity because
27 we can't listen to other people's opinions.
28
29 Be still and know that I am God
30
31 God be with you
32
33 Kingsley

Thu 7 May

Subject: LMA plump partridge

Dear All

One question I hate, when someone dies the first words out of some people's mouths is 'how old was he/ she?' Does it matter? I hate pigeon holes. What is 'a certain age'?

God has always dealt with us as individuals, who we are. In Jo-an's garden was a wheelbarrow upside down, when I went to move it some time ago I saw a nest with eggs in so carefully replaced it hoping I hadn't disturbed them.   Recently I was glad when I heard little voices calling out to be fed and knew everything was alright. Now there are lots of little sparrows back and forward to the bird table. If God cares for each of them how much more does he care for us?

Jesus called a strange assortment of people to follow him, they didn't have to reach a certain standard or pass any test, the only test was if they followed when he called because we know there were others who didn't. He didn't even call only the ones who would agree with him.

But we prefer to choose who we associate with, we like people to agree with us. I like people to disagree with me because I might be wrong. How can we learn when people don't question what we say or we are so right all the time the other person must be wrong.

1 Jesus was preparing his disciples for a journey not a
2 destination. Although he was with them at this time
3 for forty days even he could not prepare them for
4 everything, life is a journey and we learn by doing, we
5 learn from the other people we meet along the way, we
6 learn from experiences we are not used to. None of us
7 were used to the present experience and all of us are
8 having to learn.
9
10 Every blessing
11
12 Kingsley
13
14
15 **Fri 8 May**
16 Subject: LMA fat falcon
17
18 Dear All
19
20
21 To all the newbies a word of explanation, on Tuesday
22 this was a round robin and I have been going through a
23 series of overweight birds since. Also there is a website
24 eastlandsker.com but it is still under construction and
25 changes from time to time. These are not sermons or
26 thoughts for the day but the ramblings of a Vicar under
27 lockdown.
28
29 The whole of history revolves around Jesus, when God
30 came to earth and lived a human being, died and rose to
31 life again. The disciples were probably not aware that
32 they were living through such an important historical
33 event and would go on to change the world.

To a lesser extent we are living through a major
historical event. No one knew how to handle this, there
can be no experts because this has not happened before,
and as for those who tell us how society will be after -
opinion is all it is because it really hasn't happened
before and there is no experience to go by. If we have
been taking this time to listen to God then we are in a
position to make a difference and change the world for
the better, not the church, not the hierarchy, us. We are
the ones who live in the world and will once again meet
with people and it will be up to us to make the new
world a better place. We will not be sitting in ivory
towers holding meetings from a safe distance, we are
the ones in the community who the rest of the world
will see. We will make a difference because this is what
we do and who we are.

God bless you all

Kingsley

Sat 9 May

Subject: LMA bloated blackbird

Dear All

Thanks to J_

who seems to be overfeeding the birds in her garden for
since Monday's round robin she has seen a whole
variety of overweight birds, I may put the whole list on
the website.

Ahead of Boris on Sunday our First Minister has said what restrictions are lifted in Wales - not a lot, so we're in for another 3 weeks at least.

Are we getting downhearted or despondent? Not us surely. Because we know we are not in this alone and if we can save lives it is the least we can do.

And because we have faith and hope.

As I said at the beginning of the week I have been doing a lot of reflecting, as a Vicar how can I fulfil my calling? I wonder how some clergy cope for whom the communion and liturgy in central, for me (being low church) the people come first and the only way I can do that is through these emails, phone calls and talking to people 6 feet away queuing outside shops or clapping on a Thursday.

Ascension is less than two weeks away and I wonder if the disciples were feeling the time was going too fast for them and soon Jesus would leave them, mixed feelings I suppose. They would like to have him with them for ever physically but he was teaching them about the mission he had for them and perhaps they were keen to get going. Changing the world is a daunting task.

And after this, how will my mission have changed? How will church have changed? This is up to all of us, let us all play our part when things begin again.

Regards

Kingsley

Sun 10 May

Subject: LMA Easter IV

Dear All

The gospel reading today is when Peter not knowing what to do decides to go fishing - the old normal for him - and some of the others go with him. They catch nothing until the next morning Jesus, who they didn't recognise, tells them to try the other side of the boat. This leads to a large catch, them recognising him, having breakfast and eventually Jesus challenging Peter on how much he loves him. There are so many lessons here which you have all heard before. Although we are four weeks after Easter this was obviously an early meeting they had with Jesus. It does give us an idea of Jesus' teaching methods, doing something practical and asking awkward questions.

In our lockdown what sort of things have we heard from him? If they are the sort of things that go along with what we already think, if they are questions that are comfortable then it probably isn't him but our own wishful thinking. If we have been asked awkward or challenging things then we ought to listen. We cannot go back to the old normal, Peter tried and found himself challenged.

When the church opens again we are the ones who will be faced with the questions, why did so many people have to die? Where was the church when we needed it most? Do any of us know the answers?

1
2
3
4
5
6
7
8
9
10
11
12
13
14
15
16
17
18
19
20
21
22
23
24
25
26
27
28
29
30
31
32
33

Jesus asks us all, do you love me? If we do then he will tell us to feed his sheep. Whatever has happened has happened, what is gone is gone, we go forward into the new world and we are not alone, he is with us, always.

Kingsley

Mon 11 May

Subject: LMA Week 7

Dear All

Jesus may have talked to thousands at a time but he would always gather his close friends together to explain what it meant. You would have thought as he was God he would love everyone equally, well yes he does but not everyone responds equally and the really important teaching he knew he had to impart to an intimately small group.

When I was involved in the Billy Graham Mission 89 as a counsellor all the people I counselled had been brought by a church group and follow up would be done by them, again the really important teaching was done by an intimately small group.

You never know where you are with crowds, for some reason they are easily swayed.

These emails I find strangely intimate. I cannot see you but from the responses I have had it does feel very personal. I am not cleaver enough to press a button and

it goes to everyone on a list I have to type in everyone's 1
emails every time (which is why I miss some occasionally 2
- sorry) but while I do that I think of you as individuals. 3
4
You must also excuse me for my ramblings sometimes, 5
because of the strangely intimate nature of these I am 6
revealing more of myself on a personal level than 7
I would in church. It is also your responses to these that 8
are keeping me sane and I feel I am in some small way 9
still able to fulfil my calling. 10
11
So thank you for reading and thank you for your 12
support. 13
14
Kingsley 15
16

Tue 12 May 17

18
Subject: LMA analytic moraliser 19

20
Dear All 21

The world is full of contradictions. The number of 22
people still dying, the confusing message from the 23
government (at least Wales is straight forward), and the 24
increasing number of usually cheerful people who are 25
now feeling the strain. While all about us is the glory of 26
nature in all its May splendour and glory. 27
28
The time the disciples spent with Jesus after the 29
resurrection must have felt like a contradiction, he had 30
died and risen from the dead, he had defeated death 31
and Satan, and yet he was preparing them for a tough 32
mission in a hostile world. 33

1 Our present situation has taught us never to take
2 anything for granted, all the things we cannot do that
3 were so much part of life before. But as Jesus promised
4 he would be with us always the promise still holds, we
5 must depend more on him.

6
7 The glorious world around us through which God
8 shows his love and abundance reminds us there is
9 always hope and there is always joy.

10
11 God's rich blessing be on you all this day.

12
13 Kingsley

14
15 **Wed 13 May**

16
17 Subject: LMA aires romantically

18
19 Dear All

20 I keep reflecting how very lucky we are to live where we
21 do with nature bursting in full force all around us and
22 yet so many things seem unreal. This came on us so
23 suddenly even though I and a few others I know felt that
24 something was going to happen but had no idea what.

25
26 This is a testing time for so many people in so many
27 ways so I shouldn't grumble about my lot. Coming into
28 this no one knew what to expect and only with hindsight
29 will we know if the right decisions were made. Speaking
30 as a Vicar I question the sense of closing the churches, it
31 is as if even the hierarchy didn't consider them necessary.
32 Yes we can pray anywhere, yes there is technology for
33 us to keep in touch, but how will history judge?

From the early church space was set aside for the sole
purpose of gathering together for worship, they didn't
meet in kitchens or living rooms or go from house to
house, anyone who had a large enough house would
dedicate a room and that was their church building and
everyone would gather there.   Archaeologists have
found these rooms, with religious murals and often a
side room for baptism. Whatever you think people do
need a special place to feel closer to God. Strangely my
special place is not St Mary's church, rather outside the
porch facing east, if I get really personal in these emails I
may tell you why. For the moment sitting in my study
tapping away to you on the keyboard and looking at
Whitland Valley through the window is very special.

I hope you have all found your special place where you
feel close to God.

Every blessing

Kingsley

P.s. We never got to properly form a LMA council let
alone appoint a lay chair (which still sound like a
lounger to me), the Bishop would like to have a zoom
meeting with the lay chairs but as we don't have one
would anyone like to join a zoom meeting with the
Bishop - this in no way commits you to being a chair -
just to represent the LMA and find out what is going
on. This would be next week so let me know as soon as
possible. By the way you will need a computer/tablet/
smartphone with a camera and download the free
version of zoom (the cloud one) because the church has
paid to be host.

Thu 14 May

Subject: LMA eliminatory rascal

Dear All

I had to drive out of Whitland to Parc Gwyn recently, what shocked me was how strange that felt! How many of us are now living in a small world where the next town might as well be Mars. How many of us are suffering from lockdown fever and perhaps don't even realise.

We human being are adaptable and we are all finding ways to keep going and generally people are still quite cheerful. But there is an underlying fear and people are getting a little fractious (yes even me).

With Jesus departure looming I wonder how the disciples felt. I expect John would have liked Jesus to stay longer while Peter was impetuous to get on with things, and everyone else was somewhere in between.

The glory of nature all around us reminds us that as winter has given way to spring our present troubles will always give way to joy through Jesus Christ.

God be with you.

Kingsley

Fri 15 May

Subject: LMA calamari storyline

Dear All

Has anyone spotted what links all this week's subjects
(except Monday)?

Mixed messages. We have been frightened into thinking
we are all going to die or be seriously ill, we are told we
are going to have this virus for years before it is under
control, we are told the numbers of people in hospital
with it are going down, there are plans to lift the
lockdown, there are differences between Wales,
England, Scotland and Northern Ireland, we are told if
the lockdown is lifted too soon there will be second
wave, there are pictures of crowded tube trains and
busses, etc, etc.

The church has always given a mixed message and this
message seems to change according to society's current
thinking. Is there such a place as hell or isn't there?
What constitutes a sin any more? God is constant and
yet the church is like the tail trying to wag the dog.
I have been trying to get back to the basics as I am
sure you all have. If only we could sit with the disciples
and listen to Jesus directly. Even now our own preconceptions probably muddy the waters.

We have the unique opportunity now to be quiet, empty
our minds and simply be with God. We cannot see God
if we have our own picture of him in our head, we
cannot hear God if we put our own words into his
mouth. Don't reel off what you already know. God did
not cause what is happening but he will bring good out
of it if we let him, and one thing he has given us is a

wilderness to find him. Let God decide what the church will be afterwards.

Peace be with you.

Kingsley

Sat 16 May

Subject: LMA arise romantically

Dear All

What have all the subjects in the subject box have in common this week? They are all anagrams of local ministry area!

Jesus' disciples by now must have been realising the importance of the time they were living through, Jesus was preparing to leave them and tried to teach them everything they needed to know about carrying on with his mission afterwards, but had they taken it in? The promise was that he would always be with them and he would send the Holy Spirit to guide and empower them.

Normally I wouldn't have been reflecting on this period between Easter and the Ascension, life would have been too busy and there would have been too many things to organise. Easter Vestries, planning events, etc. I hadn't realised that this period was so long. We expect God to do things immediately but sometimes he needs to slow us down in order for us to learn because we are always part of his solution.

I believe he is using this period we are going through to
reach out and teach us what we need for something
important after lockdown. I hope we are listening.
Forty days is his usual time, but this is longer than that,
perhaps because we have to unlearn so much first, to
strip away preconceptions and biases before we can
hear properly. If we believe the same things as when
this began then we haven't been listening, because he is
about to do something new and none of us know what
it is.

Let go and let God.

Kingsley

Sun 17 May

Subject: LMA Easter V

Dear All

Jesus told his disciples they could ask God direct in his
name so that our joy would be complete. I am sure
there are many instances when we have done this and
not had a reply and this is one of the big problems we
face as Christians. Perhaps we are not directing the
request at God but at our idea of God, perhaps we are
not using Jesus name but our own, or perhaps our
request would not bring us joy even if we think it
would.

How can we be sure we are talking to God direct, as
I said before too often we have our idea of God. Can

we even vaguely imagine what it must be like to face God? Moses was afraid to, John found it too much to bear. The request we have, could we boldly walk into his presence and ask him face to face? Only through Jesus would we have the courage and are we sure we are being true to his command to love one another and therefore can we really be asking in his name?

And joy, do we even know what it is?

Perhaps we have a better idea now because of the lockdown. We are having to reassess what is truly important, it is not money or things but it is people, it is family and friends, it is the simple joy of meeting together and sharing.

Therefore let us come to God, in Jesus name, and ask for an end to the virus that our joy will be complete.

Amen.

Kingsley

Mon 18 May

Subject: LMA Week 8

Dear All

Have you realised several amazing things?

God created the universe and everything in it out of nothing and therefore he is in all nature and we can see his handiwork everywhere.

He sent his son into the world as a fully human being through Mary, as he created all things this is no problem for him.

He came to live and die and live again to heal the rift between us and him.

In a few days is the ascension when Jesus is taken bodily into heaven in full sight of the disciples.

The veil between us and the otherworld is more there in our inability to perceive and God is closer to us that often we realise.

We cannot say we exist in one reality and God in another, it is all part of the same reality. After all we have that nature being physical and spiritual, it is not a dual nature rather it is who we are.

Do not hide from God today.

Kingsley

Tue 19 May

Subject: LMA Ramblings

Dear All

Every day is a gift of God, it is full of possibility and even in these days when one day seems much like another it is a day further away from a dark past to a bright and hopeful future.

The worst time the disciples had to face was when Jesus was arrested, tried and executed, and for three days they suffered with dashed hope, threat of arrest themselves and loss of purpose. When Jesus rose from the dead he gave them hope and purpose again and even the threat of arrest (which would come for many of them) seemed minor compared to the joy.

With the tentative easing of lockdown we can begin to see the light at the end of the tunnel, even if this will be with us for a long time yet. I have no idea when the churches will be open again but we are still here for the church is us. I have been doing a lot of reflecting during this time and reading your responses so have you, when we can perhaps it would be good to get together in person and share our experiences of lockdown because I am sure many of us have come a long way.

I look forward to sharing in person.

Kingsley

Wed 20 May

Subject: LMA meanderings

Dear All

Jesus warned his disciples that he was sending them out as sheep among wolves, they would face many dangers for although the message is of love and joy and hope there are always some who do not want any of that. Even though the battle had been won there is still

darkness in the world.   But he encouraged them by 1
saying that he had overcome the world, he would be 2
with them always, and if they kept going there was joy 3
at the end. 4

5

During this period many people have shown themselves 6
up, the selfish, the hateful, but more than that the self- 7
giving, the generous, those willing to risk even their 8
own lives for others.   Always remember there are so 9
many more good people than bad. 10

11

When we emerge from hibernation and blink in the 12
light of freedom we will feel invigorated, this will be a 13
good opportunity to show who we really are and dispel 14
the fear that many people will still be feeling. 15

16

Regards 17

18

Kingsley 19

20

21

22

23

24

25

26

27

28

29

30

31

32

33

Part 5 Ascension

Thu 21 May

Subject: LMA rabbiting away

Dear Pilgrims

Today Jesus was taken into heaven before their eyes. They didn't need to discuss this or work out the theology of it they saw it happen. He promised he would be with them always and told them to wait in Jerusalem until they were empowered by the Holy Spirit to be witnesses to the ends of the earth. He had taught them all they needed to know, they had seen amazing things, surely now everything was possible, they just had to wait a little longer.

And we wait too. Having had a zoom meeting yesterday with the Archdeacon and other LMA deans I have some idea of the churches plans to end our lockdown. When the churches can be open don't expect it to be suddenly like it used to be, at first there will be social distancing, only churches with a way in and a separate way out will open first, probably no communion to begin with, no singing because singing spreads germs much further. You all need to look at your churches, is there a separate way out? Is there enough space for the congregation to be six feet apart (or have they always done this anyway!) Would it be wise for the Vicar to go from church to church? In churches with lay worship leaders you already have the solution. And this is just worship,

1 when we will be able to visit one another may take
2 longer.
3
4 Unlike the disciples who after Pentecost were launched
5 suddenly into their ministry we will have to ease our
6 way back.
7
8 As soon as I can, and weather permitting I intend to
9 hold an open air service at St Mary's, it will be an
10 informal service to reflect on what we have learned,
11 pray for those who have died, and to gather together at
12 a safe distance as the worshiping people of God. Sadly
13 I have no date.
14
15 Keep safe, keep well.
16
17 Kingsley
18
19
20 **Fri 22 May**
21 Subject: LMA perambulations
22
23 Dear Fellow Hermits
24
25 Peter takes charge, having been told by Jesus that he
26 was the rock on which the church would be built and
27 told to feed his sheep what is the first thing he does? He
28 holds a meeting (you would think he was Anglican)
29 to decide who should replace Judas. They decided on
30 two names, prayed and drew lots! Matthias was chosen
31 and we never hear anything about him in the Bible
32 again. Much later God chooses Saul changing his name
33 to Paul.

How do we distinguish between what God actually
wants and what we think he wants? One or two people
I know are sure they can but I can't, I have to struggle
on doing what I hope is best and leave plenty of room
for God to do his own thing anyway. We each of us
have to do the best we can and act according to our
beliefs, but ultimately it is God who will take our best
efforts and make something of them. We need to be
humble enough not to get in his way when he acts and
ready to join in with him when he does.

We are still in hermit mode at the moment but I hope we
are beginning to feel ready for the work God has for us.

Every blessing

Kingsley

By the way, the re-opening of churches is unlikely before
July! Could I have a list of churches with two doors
please.

How many of you would like a zoom service before
then?

Sat 23 May

Subject: LMA walkabout

Dear Fellow Seekers

The other thing the disciples did after the ascension and
before Pentecost was continually meet in the temple to

praise God. Even without the coming of the Holy Spirit they no longer feared arrest but met openly.

There has been so much fear over COVID-19 that one thing we need to do once we can meet again is to meet with joy and put fear behind us. Now, I am not saying we should throw caution to the wind, after all it seems some ministers in the bible belt of America have believed that they were exempt because of their faith and many of them have died of the virus. We still have to be sensible and abide by the guidelines that are given. Also many people have died and there is that underlying sadness and we do need to remember them, and remember all the hard work and sacrifice of all those who have kept things going.

But Pentecost is almost upon us, the birth of the church, and let us hope it will be a new birth for us too.

Regards

Kingsley

Sun 24 May

Subject: LMA Sunday after Ascension

Dear Friends

During this period between the Ascension and Pentecost I expect the disciples reflected a lot on the things Jesus said, perhaps one of the things was what we have in today's reading about Jesus prayer for them just before he was arrested. As I have often said people seem to

assume that God is so nice everyone will enter eternal
life, yes Jesus came to break the power of death and
offer eternal life but in this prayer we are reminded that
he will give eternal life to those the Father has given
him, and that he doesn't pray for the world, because he
knows that he will be rejected and so will his message.

There is the worry that the churches having been closed
during this time will people come back when eventually
they reopen, sadly for some going to church can be a habit
which they have now got out of. Will many people who
have found an alternative online find it too convenient to
continue? We can but wait and see. One thing that is
important though is the fellowship of worshiping together,
and Christianity is not just a private thing between us and
God it is how we are with each other, after all what good
is your Christianity if no one knows? If people's faith is
genuine we will see them back in church, even if we only
have a few, Jesus started with 12, and a committed few is
a strong base to rebuild the church.

Every blessing

Kingsley

Mon 25 May

Subject: LMA week 9

Dear Friends

My apologies if sometimes I am a bit negative in these
emails but when I get messages from the bishop's office

on the one hand saying she is concerned with the mental health of the clergy and then a whole list of don'ts and don'ts for when the churches will tentatively open (which isn't yet anyway) it is enough to get even the most optimistic down.

Therefore, switching to positive mode.

Jesus disciples are still meeting in the temple to worship God and then going back to the upper room to meet together. Where they met in the temple was a large open air public place, many of the stall holders were probably still annoyed and would be eyeing the disciples with suspicion, it is a wonder the authorities allowed it, but then we don't know how many disciples were there probably a lot more than the eleven. And they waited, it isn't recorded whether Jesus told them how long they should wait but there was the festival of Pentecost coming up and they probably thought that was significant.

Perhaps Pentecost will be significant for us too. Never forget that God is full of surprises and I wouldn't put it past him to do something on a day other than Pentecost but still in the near future.

Regards

Kingsley

Tue 26 May

Subject: LMA letter

Dear Friends

I find I contradict myself an awful lot, I am not a patient 1
person and like to get on with things, and yet I am quite 2
at ease with all this waiting we have to do at the 3
moment. I like to make things up as I go along and be 4
spontaneous, but I also like a structure and routine to 5
my life. This letter has become part of the routine and I 6
wonder what I would do with myself when it becomes 7
unnecessary. How easily we get into routines. 8

9

The disciple's new routine is now worshiping in the 10
temple and meeting in the upper room. They knew they 11
were waiting for the Holy Spirit but they had no idea 12
what that was about, how they would know when he 13
came and what they would do when he did. They didn't 14
have our advantage of hindsight. 15

16

But we do not have the advantage of hindsight for our 17
present situation. We know things will change, the 18
churches will open, we also know that God has been 19
preparing us by making us face ourselves, yet we don't 20
know what it is all leading to. 'The old has gone, let it 21
go. Behold I do a new thing'. 22

23

Kingsley 24

25

26

Wed 27 May 27

Subject: LMA epistle 28

29

Dear Friends 30

31

It feels like it ought to be August or September but it is 32
still only May, I'm sure this is the longest year on record. 33

Looking out of my study window I can look across part of Whitland Valley, less now because the trees are in full leaf, and I can't help reflecting how many people have come and gone since people lived here and the land remains. Whether our time is long or short we are only passing through, so how can we possibly understand the prospect of eternal life? I have often said that the Bible isn't primarily about the next life it is about how to live in this. We may have promises and we may have hopes but God intended for us to live in this world, to make the most of this life and do our best for one another while we are here. Jesus wanted his disciples to have joy and he wasn't talking about the next life but this - do you know how many times joy is mentioned in the Bible?

The life we have now is a gift, he has given us a beautiful world to live in. I may not have lived here all my life but I feel I belong, I am part of the valley itself and spring is a time when nature itself breathes new life through us. With Pentecost approaching let God breathe new life through us all.

Regards

Kingsley

Thu 28 May

Subject: LMA missive

Dear Friends

The lockdown has certainly given me a new perspective
on the times between events such as Easter, Ascension
and Pentecost, times that with the normal business
I would have skipped over. I am reflecting on the time
the disciples waited for the Holy Spirit, worshiping in
the temple, meeting in the upper room, Peter now in
charge.

And Peter was a fisherman. The trouble with any
organisation and this goes for the church too, is that
you have to work your way up to the important
positions, you have to attend the right meetings and get
to know the right people and as a result you lose touch
with the real people in the real world. We are in our
communities, we know the joys and sorrows of those
around us, the hopes and the fears. Where the church
goes and what it is therefore is up to us. We now have a
blank canvas, let us paint on it what the Holy Spirit
inspires us to paint and what we believe, let us make a
new and beautiful picture.

Regards

Kingsley

Fri 29 May

Subject: LMA postcard

Dear Friends

Yesterday I took a trip down to the recycling centre,
only now during lockdown is this news! How strange

this period is! So many things we used to take for granted are no longer part of our lives. I have said the church will not be the same but really it is everything, the world, our way of life.

And yet, nature is full of glory (though rather dry through lack of rain and a little brighter through lack of pollution). The world itself it largely unchanged, rather it is the people who have changed. If you look back through history there have been so many major events that have changed the people and we never expected to live through such a time now.

And God hasn't changed either. Our perception of him may have because we have been forced to get closer to ourselves and closer to him, he has been able to get through the noise of our busy lives and speak to us in the quiet. It is worth reflecting on the people we were on March 22 and the people we are now, all that we have learned, how we have changed. And still this is not yet over. As the lockdown slowly eases we will probably really appreciate each new little freedom as it comes, so let us enjoy the little things as they happen.

With the disciples it was BANG and everything changes, God never repeats himself and for us it will be gradual and bit by bit. Don't expect a mighty wind and flames of fire, expect a gentle breeze and a warming of our hearts.

Kingsley

Sat 30 May

Subject: LMA notelet

Dear Friends

I am a bit later this morning because we have just gone for a long walk along the roman road. The weather is still keeping glorious! There always seem to be compensations, during this dreadful period the weather is the best it has been for years so people have been able to get out, imagine what it would have been like if it had been cold and raining all this time.

I have been finding this time a very spiritually refreshing time. As I have often repeated I would normally be busy, the church year tends to push you on to the next thing all the time. I have had time to reflect on what Jesus' disciples were doing day by day, the times they waited but they didn't sit at home twiddling their thumbs, they were still going to the temple every day to worship.

We may not be able to go to the church but we are so lucky here that God in nature is all around and he can reach out to us in the temple of his world as long as we are open enough to let him into our hearts.

I expect you all have stories of how God has spoken to you at this time and I would love to hear these stories and perhaps we can share them when we can meet together in the open air outside the church.

Every blessing

Kingsley

1
2
3
4
5
6
7
8
9
10
11
12
13
14
15
16
17
18
19
20
21
22
23
24
25
26
27
28
29
30
31
32
33

Part 6 Pentecost

Sun 31 May

Subject: LMA Pentecost

Dear Friends

The disciples were gathered together and the Holy Spirit came with the sound of a wind and what appeared to be tongues of flame on everyone head. Over the ages what does the church do but gives bishops pointy hats.

There is an air of expectancy this year but if you are hoping the Holy Spirit will rush onto us all, empower us and we just go along for the ride then I fear you may be disappointed. Today is not THE Day of Pentecost, we already have the Holy Spirit and if he was going to empower us we already are. God is already working in us if we have taken this opportunity to let him, he is already speaking to us if we have been quiet enough to listen.

The disciples were suddenly unleashed onto the world, starting in Jerusalem, the people were ready to hear and the church grew rapidly. Wonders and miracles abounded.

For the Celtic church miracles were simply part of the natural world and if we have taken time to look at the natural world around us we know the power of God and when we fully grasp that then miracles will follow.

Be open to the Holy Spirit and he will guide you and we will see miracles.

Every blessing

Kingsley

Mon 1 June

Subject: LMA Week 10

Dear Friends

Today we are given a little more freedom, two house-holds can meet at a distance, we can begin to see there will be an end to this. As soon as enough people can meet outside at a distance we can at least have an open air service or services at your own churches. I am not even going to think about the weather.

The disciples being launched into the world did everything in the open air, that is how they managed to reach out to so many so quickly. We miss our churches deeply but have we done too much safely behind closed doors? Not that they were closed there was always a welcome but it meant people had to come to us. Perhaps our first move is to worship in public? This may mean a certain amount of ridicule and perhaps some of us will find it a little embarrassing, but it is worth a thought.

And this is not yet, we are still waiting and listening to God, and our only witness is while queuing for shops and chatting to the people six feet in front and behind

and asking the people serving in shops how they are
today. Don't underestimate the importance of chatting
to people in the street, we are all communities and it is
through the community that Christ's message is spread.

Every blessing

Kingsley

Tue 2 June

Subject: LMA reflection

Dear friends

We need a little magic now and then. Humans have this
capacity to step outside of themselves and to imagine
and to dream. This is where great art, music, poetry,
stories come from. But we all have this ability.

Acts 2:17b 'Your sons and daughters will prophesy,
your young men will see visions, your old men will
dream dreams.'

It is not enough to plan for coming out of lockdown, to
prepare our churches safely. We need a vision. With all
the dullness of what we can't do (such as singing, sit
near each other, share the peace, etc., etc.) we need
magic. We need something positive to give us something
to be excited about.

The early church was excited and somehow our
'modern' church has lost this excitement. I am excited

because the future is an 'undiscovered country' and God is doing a new thing.

We cannot rely on technology, though it has been a boon of late, because there is an enormous solar flare which means a lot more activity in the sun which may disrupt signals and satellites.

I wait eagerly to see what God is doing, but I am not sitting on my bottom leaving it all to him, I have my ideas.

God's rich blessing on you all

Kingsley

Wed 3 June

Subject: LMA cogitation

Dear Friends

Apart from meeting regularly for teaching, fellowship, breaking of bread and prayer in a group much more than just the apostles everything else was done without planning. Peter and John were passing a beggar who asked for money and Peter simply healed him, when they were called before the Sanhedrin they just spoke what they believed.

I remember the decade of evangelism but how long did it last, I remember vision 2020 so where was the vision in that? One thing we can learn from our present situation is that God obviously doesn't sit in on meetings and does his own thing anyway. Coming out of lock-down is not something any of us have experience of therefore can we really plan?

Now more than ever we must act as the Holy Spirit guides us. He is not going to ask us to do anything that will put anyone in danger but what he does prompt us to will be unexpected and perhaps a little strange.

The Holy Spirit will not go against our free will either, we can ignore his prompting or we can take the risk and follow his guidance. If we are to see wonders we must be open and dare to be different.

Every blessing

Kingsley

Thu 4 June

Subject: LMA cogitation

Dear Friends

As the early believers experienced the power of the Holy Spirit, enabling them to see wonders and miracles, and as they shared everything you would expect everything to be wonderful. But Ananias and Sapphira kept something back, which they had a right to do, rather it was the lie they were condemned for. It is a sobering thought that you can hide nothing from God.

During this lockdown we have all had to face ourselves and I hope you have found strength in this that you didn't know you had, but this required honesty, honesty with yourself and honesty with God. After all you are the person God made you to be, you are special to him and loved by him, and you need to find within yourself that which is unique and wonderful. We are not expected to be the face we put on to others at the moment, we are free to be truly ourselves.

When we begin to gather together again we will all have something precious to bring back to our friends, so don't put on your old public face, be the person you are.

Every blessing

Kingsley

Fri 5 June

Subject: LMA rumination

Dear Friends

It certainly wasn't all sweetness and light at the beginning of the church, Grecian Jews were complaining against Hebraic Jews that their widows were being overlooked when the daily food was distributed. Taking the complaint to the apostles they were too important to see to it so seven deacons were appointed to sort out trivial matters. So where was Jesus example of washing feet? Even with the years of Jesus' teaching and example,

even with the coming of the Holy Spirit, human pride is
still there.

It is good to know that there are those in our
communities who aren't too important to help others in
need, those who are following the example Jesus set.
Even though we have been given a little more freedom
the lockdown is still dragging on, but I suspect that
those who are more ready to help others find it less of a
burden themselves.   Certainly the communities have
become stronger at this time so let us hope we will not
forget each other as we are given more freedom.

Every blessing

Kingsley

Sat 6 June

Subject: LMA pondering

Dear All

Once again God has other plans. Stephen was appointed
as a deacon to do all the mundane things the apostles
were too important to do. Many wonders and miracles
were done through him, he was taken before the
Sanhedrin who were so incensed by his preaching to
them that they stoned him to death, and as he died he
saw heaven open and God waiting for him.

Who we are will always shine through no matter what
job we do, no matter how ordinary. Stephen was the

first martyr and the Church eventually celebrated him on the day after Christmas. The job we do or the position we hold, our wealth or rank or importance in Earthly terms is nothing compared to the esteem God has for us. In a way Stephen was responsible for the eventual conversion of Paul. We may never know the effect we have on other people, we should always be ourselves and if we are true to what God asks of us he will use us to change the hearts of those around us.

Blessings

Kingsley

Sun 7 June

Subject: LMA Trinity

Dear Friends

God never was a local god, and although the Jews were a chosen people we wasn't just concerned with them. God is Maker of All Things and he gave everyone the chance to find him. When he sent his Son into the world he arranged everything right, he prepared the world for his coming. And so the pieces were all in place so the world could understand. The Jews had the promise and the tradition, the Greeks had the philosophy and the Celts had the spirituality (though this is probably an over simplification). When it comes to understanding the Trinity the Jews could not accept this even though the doctrine is there throughout the old testament, it took the Greek philosophy of knowing a

perfection beyond the physical that everything in this
world is only a copy of and the Celtic spiritual understanding of the natural world which is both physical
and spiritual and the importance of a threefold God in
his dealings with all of creation.

Do not limit God to your own understanding of him
and do not write off other people's understanding as in
error because they don't agree with you. None of us are
all knowing, none of us are clever enough to understand
everything there is about God. We can only know in
part, our experience of Him is unique to us but it is not
the only experience. One of my great joys is that I can
never know everything, I can always be surprised by
God doing something new and unexpected. I have no
preconceptions about the church as it will be, I know
people are worried if their church will survive but I just
do not know. The future is an undiscovered country
and whatever God's plans are no one knows. I have
often wondered how anyone can be an expert on
COVID-19 and how it will all work out when it is all
unknown, so how can we know how the church is going
to work out as no one can possibly be an expert on that.

That doesn't mean I am simply going to sit here and
wait for God to do something. I will use whatever
lessening of the lock down we are allowed to start using
the churches again as soon as possible and then see
where God leads us.

God's blessings to you all

Kingsley

Mon 8 June

Subject: LMA Week 11

Dear Friends

I have always thought stuff like mobile phones and internet were somehow magical or mysterious. When typing in all your emails I sometimes get them wrong and a few minutes after sending it the MAILER-DAEMON brings it back (which is why sometimes you get missed). It isn't a particular spelling of Demon (an evil spirit) rather a Daemon is a benevolent or benign earth spirit, so are earth spirits really behind delivering emails? I asked an earth spirit of my acquaintance and she was amused that we humans have such strange ideas, earth spirits don't do technology.

Technology has been so useful during the lockdown but it does not fully compensate for the lack of human contact. I miss sitting and having a coffee and a chat so how must it be for the bereaved and lonely? The wonders of nature all around us remind us that God is still active in the world and he is a consolation to those of us who have opened the door. But we are still social animals and we need contact with one another, even hermits in the desert would have people come to them for wisdom and teaching, and this is an unseen harm that it is going to take a long time to get over. Even when lockdown ends the virus will still be there and people will still be wary. Yet it is only one of many viruses and many dangers in the world and we cannot

live in fear for ever, when the time comes let go of fear
and learn to live again.

Bless you all

Kingsley

1
2
3
4
5
6
7
8
9
10
11
12
13
14
15
16
17
18
19
20
21
22
23
24
25
26
27
28
29
30
31
32
33

Part 7 Slow Opening

Tue 9 June

Subject: LMA hello

Dear Friends

For all the new friends, try out eastlandsker.com

I have had permission from the Bishop to enter the church but with an eye to assessing distancing etc., but still at least I can go in. She has also checked with the legal bods and under the Welsh regulations that two households can get together outside at a distance clergy are counted as one of the households so I can visit parishioners outside, bearing in mind the virus is still with us so for your safety and for mine and Jo-an's I am not going to go overboard with this. If someone <u>needs</u> to see me then we can follow the guidelines, it is not enough just to think 'wouldn't it be nice to see the Vicar'. No tea and cakes!

In case you have passed Y Ficerdy and have been wondering at the wilderness that is the lawn the Diocese have told me they will do the first two cuts of the lawn but neglected to say when so don't think it's me being lazy, also the ground is still rough so an ordinary lawnmower probably couldn't do it. However it is a haven for wildlife and there is a certain beauty in wildness. Sometimes our lives can be a little too ordered, a little too neat. Nature isn't neat and tidy, there is a sort of celebration in abandonment and surely it shows that if our idea of God is neat and tidy then we have got him wrong. God doesn't conform to our ideas of him, nothing is cut and dried, we cannot limit him, we cannot put him in a box. As C. S. Lewis said in the Narnia books, Aslan is not a tame lion. I will never claim to know what he wants or what he is telling me to do, I will just do what I feel is right and trust him to make something of it. These emails are an example, they sort of happened by accident and were never (by me anyway) meant to be what they have become, so as lockdown restrictions are lifted I won't know when to stop but when they do I will miss them.

Bless you all for your forbearance!

Kingsley

Wed 10 June

Subject: LMA greetings

Dear Friends

Thank you for all your kind emails yesterday, I take that as a loud and clear message not to stop these emails! Not that I intended to just yet anyway rather I will keep on until they are no longer necessary which is still probably months away.

I mentioned C.S. Lewis the other day being a fan of his, and I find that he and J.R.R. Tolkien both being very Christian men seemed to understand the magic and

indeed the very life in nature around us. Many of the 1
human problems we have given ourselves are because we 2
too often see nature as a commodity to be used. We do 3
not understand the spirituality in nature because it is all 4
part of the loving creation of God or even our attachment 5
to nature because our very molecules are the same - dust 6
we are and unto dust shall we return. For those of us 7
who have eyes to see beyond ourselves and selfish wants 8
we have seen how very fragile humanity is for all its 9
boasting and bluster, we have all been stopped in our 10
tracks to reassess what is important. Sadly for some it 11
seems lounging on a beach or queuing for hours for a 12
McDonalds! I hope we have found a peace and a 13
strength within ourselves that is far more important than 14
things, and I hope we have found a deeper relationship 15
with God in the peace and the still small voice. 16
17
God be with you. 18
19
Kingsley 20
21
22
Thu 11 June 23

Subject: LMA salutation 24
25
Dear Friends 26
27
I went into St Mary's this morning hoping for a quiet 28
five minutes when the angel who is there asked where I 29
had been all this time, I tried to explain about social 30
distancing, COVID-19, etc., and that the Archbishop of 31
Canterbury had said clergy weren't allowed to enter the 32
churches, the angel thought I meant Augustine and had 33

never heard of Justin Welby. However angels are never exactly where they are, they appear to be somewhere but they are always in the presence of God and God must have explained things. The angel was still wondering why I was going about with a tape measure.

This got me thinking. Yes we as physical beings are restricted to where we can go and who we can meet up with, and the internet is a wonderful tool but cannot replace physical contact. But we are spiritual too and as such on the spiritual level we are not restricted and whether it is six feet, Pendine, Clydau, Snowdonia, Bristol, Luton, Canada or wherever we can be together on a level the world doesn't know. Each morning I can reach out to you all as I tap in your email addresses and these ramblings and I do feel I am reaching out spiritually too.

After all, we are the people of God and we are the church.

Kingsley

Fri 12 June

Subject: LMA hi there

Dear Friends

Cornelius, a Roman Centurion, had a vision where he was told to send for Simon Peter. Meanwhile Peter was having his own visions, he saw a large sheet coming down from heaven with all sorts of what he as a Jew

would consider unclean animals and was told to kill 1
and eat, but being a good Jew he wouldn't and God told 2
him not to call anything unclean that God had made 3
pure. This was to prepare him for the invitation to go 4
to Cornelius' house to tell him the good news. God 5
went to great lengths to persuade the early disciples to 6
go beyond the narrow confines of their own belief and 7
out into the greater world. 8
9
Have we too long been confined to our little world, 10
expecting to save the world from the safety of our 11
churches. During this period we are being given a 12
chance to reassess our own beliefs and prejudices. 13
When we can go back to church do we want it to be as 14
it was? Or is this the opportunity we need to start 15
afresh with a new vision, to make of the church 16
something new and different. I have said before, God 17
did not cause this it is of human making, but he will use 18
it to bring something positive out of it. What sort of a 19
church do we want? What sort of a church does God 20
want? And what sort of a church does the world need? 21
22
Kingsley 23
24
25
Sat 13 June
26
Subject: LMA felicitations 27
28
Dear Friends 29
30
I had a message from the Bishop, it is hoped that 31
churches may be open for personal prayer from 22nd 32
June, but no services, no gathering, no singing, no 33

1 speaking at the same time (such as even reciting the
2 Lord's prayer together). So if people want to go into the
3 church just to pray (as long as the church has passed
4 the requirements) they can but I am sure we have all
5 been praying anyway wherever we are. The churches
6 are special though, in that they are places where there
7 has been worship and prayer through the ages and
8 people will find comfort in being able to go there.
9
10 When I was young we lived in England (well someone
11 has to) but would come to Tenby for holidays and we
12 were always looking for the sea over the next hill or
13 round the next corner. We have come to a corner now
14 but we haven't come to the sea, we are not there yet but
15 at least we are on a journey.
16
17 When we do have services what sort of services can we
18 have with no singing, no responses, no sharing of items,
19 so no Communion and not even a proper Matins. I
20 have some preparation to do then and so have many of
21 you, what sort of worship can we have together when
22 we can? Let us be innovative, let us try new things, let
23 us be fresh and exciting.
24
25 Every blessing
26
27 Kingsley
28
29 **Sun 14 June**
30
31 Subject: Trinity I
32
33 Dear Friends

In the green book the gospel reading is about the rich man and Lazarus. Everyone knows this parable, how the rich man did nothing for the poor man during his lifetime yet while in torment in hell he wanted Lazarus to come down from heaven even if it was just to cool his tongue with water. But Abraham points out there is a chasm between them, nor can Lazarus return to earth to warn his brothers. What is done is done.

Yet how many people still do nothing to help one another? How many people talk about doing something but leave it too late? We cannot turn back time or reset the past. We are here now and we must do the right thing now. One thing we have seen certainly locally during this lockdown is the number of people who have helped others, who haven't just sat on their behinds and moaned about their own situation. Whatever else we have learned during this time we have learned how much we need each other and how important community is, and when slowly the restrictions lessen let us hold on to our community and remember how vital this has been when things were difficult.

Look after yourselves and one another

Kingsley

Mon 15 June

Subject: LMA week 12

Dear Friends

Some say the lockdown is easing too fast in England, some say it is too slow in Wales, who can really say? Only time will tell and history will judge.

There is a proverb that is said to be Chinese but there is no proof that it is, 'May you live in interesting times'. I have always wanted to live in interesting times! But not at the cost of so many lives, it shows you must be careful what you wish for. However these are interesting times and a future historical time that people will write about and have their opinions on. Like WWII, those who lived through it often had a different impression than the historians who look back. Our experience is unique and it is our own, I will be interested to hear the experiences of others after the event over a coffee and cake. This is a big event that is changing the way we think because in so many instances we are having to face ourselves and for those of us who believe we are facing God in a deeper way too.

I hope you will excuse me if I don't get involved in other world events, I am a simple country Vicar trying to brighten up the day for a few people and simply keep in touch and this is my concern at the moment.

Have an interesting day

Kingsley

Tue 16 June

Subject: LMA Carrier Pigeon

Dear Friends

The first disciples of Jesus were all local people, they
were related to half the people in their villages, even
Jerusalem was like the other end of the world to them.
But Jesus had brought them to Jerusalem where they
settled after Easter through to Pentecost and were by
now comfortable enough to remain. Until the stoning
of Stephen and the persecution of the church, this drove
them out into the wider world - or at least Israel and the
surrounding countries.

People in those days did know about distant parts, there
were traders who travelled all over the known world
well before the Romans, but for the ordinary people like
the early Christians the prospect of taking the Gospel
to all nations must have seemed a daunting task, the
world was so vast and travel to these distant places
would have taken months and the people there were
so foreign. Yet Christianity did spread, for God had
already been there, he had prepared the way and he
travelled with them.

I mentioned recently that the future is an 'undiscovered
country' (a quote from Shakespeare), not even traders
have been there and for us it is a complete unknown.
But God is already there, he is preparing the way and he
is traveling with us. We are all pioneers traveling into
the unknown, trust in God and the future is bright and
exciting, he is doing something new and invites us to do
something new along with him.

God is with you

Kingsley

Wed 17 June

Subject: LMA pony express

Dear Friends

Practical first. I was in a zoom meeting with the Archdeacon yesterday, hopefully the First Minister will include the opening of churches for private prayer in his Friday announcement, if so the details you need are on eastlandsker.com under Miscellany, which I will continue to update when I know more.

But this email is not a practical one. It is my rambling away as I continue my inner journey during these unusual times. I have left a few breadcrumbs in these emails that the eagle eyed might have picked up on that reveal something more than face value. But I hope we are all on an inner journey and have had the space to learn something more about ourselves and even to hear God speak to us.

One of the things the coming of the Holy Spirit did for the early Christians was to take away their fear and timidity. But for them this was a sudden revelation with wind and fire and a sudden revelation. For us we have had the Holy Spirit dwelling in us to teach and inspire for so long he has been pushed away in the wardrobe of our hearts and minds like a comfortable pair of shoes rather than let him challenge us daily. In the confessions we repeat weekly in church services we not only repent of our sins but also of what we have not done and during this time I keep asking myself 'what have I not done for the Kingdom?'

The church after lockdown will be a different church
and it is up to all of us to make something new and
exciting that will reach out to the wider community, we
are a team not a one man band. When we are permitted
to hold an open air service I certainly don't intend to do
all the talking but let us see where the Spirit leads.

God be with you

Kingsley

Thu 18 June

Subject: LMA smoke signals

Dear Friends

As Philip (one of the deacons) was walking along a
chariot was passing with an Ethiopian high ranking
administrator in it. The Ethiopian was reading in Isaiah
about the suffering servant and didn't understand it.
Philip took the opportunity and offered to explain,
climbing into the chariot he explained that the passage
was about Jesus and told him all about what had
happened. They came to some water and the Ethiopian
wanted to be baptised. Thus the good news was taken
back to Ethiopia. This was not planned by Philip or the
Ethiopian but God had prepared everything.

We cannot plan for the future of the church because we
just do not know, we cannot be too rigid in what we
want to happen or expect to happen. If God is working,
which he is, then we have to be completely open to

1 where His Holy Spirit leads us and the opportunities he
2 puts before us. I may be wrong but I personally do not
3 think 'online' is the answer because it allows too much
4 anonymity and not enough real commitment though it
5 has been necessary during this period, the spreading of
6 the gospel is person to person and it is who we are when
7 we begin to mix again and more about our daily lives
8 and physically gathering together. Whatever it is God is
9 already there and he will take us by the hand and lead
10 us into the new world.

11
12 Trust in God
13
14 Kingsley
15

16 **Fri 19 June**
17
18 Subject: LMA semaphore
19
20 Dear Friends
21
22 The mark of a Christian is not how well we know the
23 Bible but how well we live it.
24 Kingsley
25
26
27 **Sat 20 June**
28 Subject: LMA news flash
29
30 Dear Friends
31
32 I am on my way to St Mary's to meet with Roger and
33 Mike to plan for opening on Wednesday for private

prayer. But we have been praying anyway and cannot
wait to meet together for fellowship.

Going back to Philip and the Ethiopian it is interesting
what they didn't do. They didn't meet with any of the
apostles, or attend any sort of service, the Ethiopian
simply went home and spread the good news straight
away. We have no way of really knowing how far and
how fast Christianity spread because we only have the
book of Acts and official records. There is the tradition
that Thomas went to India and spread the gospel there.

The established church is so fond of numbers (bums on
pews or in these days the number of people watching
services online) but we have no real idea just how many
Christians there are in the world. Jesus said whoever is
not against us is with us. There is more faith about than
sometimes our narrow interpretation allows, only God
knows truly those who believe.

Regards

Kingsley

Sun 21 June

Subject: LMA Trinity 2

Dear Friends

Call me old fashioned but I still use the CinW 1984
green book! The New Testament reading in that is from
Hebrews where the writer compares the time when

1 Moses received the ten commandments on a mountain
2 with fire and gloom and tempest to how things are now
3 - 'But you have come to Mount Zion and to the city of
4 the living God, the heavenly Jerusalem, and to
5 innumerable angels in festal gathering, and to the
6 assembly of the first-born who are enrolled in heaven
7 ...' all thanks to Jesus' sacrifice of himself. When we
8 gather together as a fellowship be it in our churches, in
9 an open air service, or even over the internet we should
10 be aware that we have come to Mount Zion, we should
11 be aware of the gathering of all those who have gone
12 before, of all the angels and of God, Father Son and
13 Holy Spirit. When you read this doesn't matter because
14 time is not important to God for we are a fellowship
15 even through this means, take a moment now to know
16 we are on Mount Zion.
17
18 God be with you, and the heavenly host and all those
19 we miss.
20
21 Kingsley
22
23
24
25
26
27
28
29
30
31
32
33

Part 8 Further Opening

Mon 22 June

Subject: LMA week 13

Dear Friends

First as there is no LMA council I can't ask agreement of the LMA council to open churches but as there are representatives of all 15 churches on this email does anyone object to opening St Mary's, Whitland and Mynachlogddu? If no one objects I will take it as agreement to go ahead.

I can't help feeling the contrast between the beginnings of Christianity and now, although there were periods of waiting when things happened they happened suddenly. In Paul's case although he was brought to a halt on the road to Damascus he still had to wait three days because God had to cram so much in, he had so much old stuff to unlearn before learning new stuff. But we wait for so long, 13 weeks so far and the end is not yet, so do we still have things to learn? Looking at reports of crowds on beaches and in shops I wonder if humanity as a whole has learned anything.

We are salt and light in the world and we can only be true to God's calling and I am sure we do make a difference. Our mission is still the same but how we go about it has changed and we will only find out by doing. Hopefully we have found a peace with God during this time and are closer now than we were and will be able to hear his voice as he leads into the future.

Every blessing

Kingsley

Tue 23 June

Subject: LMA awakening

Dear Friends

It was a dangerous time for the early Christians. James, the brother of John was killed by Herod and Peter was put in prison with the intention of killing him too. But through the combined prayer of everyone Peter was released from prison by an angel. They knew who the enemy was and they knew what to pray for and they believed.

Our enemies are mainly unseen. Quite apart from the virus there is apathy and selfishness. How do we pray against that? We could pray for the end of the virus but would the rest of the world know it was our prayers and would they thank us or God for it? A miracle needs to be seen to come from God. And how do you pray against apathy and selfishness in the world? You pray specific prayers, you pray for individuals, you pray for one at a time.

Regards

Kingsley

Wed 24 June

Subject: LMA bestirring

Dear Friends

A lot of the rest of the Book of Acts are Paul's missionary journeys and we don't hear much about everyone else, not in the Bible anyway, though there are traditions of the travels of some of the others. This is because Luke wrote Acts and he spent a lot of time with Paul, and Luke was a Greek Doctor. History is often down to who wrote it.

One of the things I was told at Theological College was that although the Bible is a complete book (or books) as it is there is a sense that it has never been completed. We, every one of us, are still writing it. Our stories, our experiences of God, our meeting with others and passing on the good news are still additions to the Bible. Today is a new chapter in the ongoing Bible so let us add valuable things to it because even if no one else reads what we do it is written in God's heart.

Every blessing

Kingsley

Thu 25 June

Subject: LMA rousing

Dear Friends

The LMA is open! As you all know the LMA is one parish so if one church is open the whole LMA is open. St Mary's was open yesterday for private prayer (thanks to Mike) and even though only he and I were there the point was made, and I was in black with a collar as I did my bit of shopping after so Whitland knew we were back. So St Mary's will be open again on Sunday from 11.00 to 12.00. Let us hope Mynachlogddu will open soon as well to cover the wilds of the north.

The early church had an enormous task, a boatful of people from a tiny country on the far shore of the Mediterranean were charged with changing the world and we are heirs to that. Time for us to do our bit, let us change the world together. But we are not alone, the Church is already widespread and God is with us.

God is with you all

Kingsley

Fri 26 June

Subject: LMA de-hibernating

Dear Friends

If you have wondered about the reality of hell then we had the pictures of Dante's Inferno on Bournmouth beach and the people who chose to be there.

On a brighter note among the recipients of this email are a couple who are now grandparents and another couple celebrating their Ruby Wedding this weekend, congratulations all round. Life goes on and there are always things to celebrate even during difficult times like this. God will always give us reasons for joy.

God loves everyone unconditionally, and this is the message behind 1 Corinthians 13, it is perfect love and it is often used at weddings because the couple at that point want genuinely to aspire to that. God also accepts that our love does not always match his as we saw when Jesus was talking to Peter by the lake after the resurrection, and yet nothing will diminish his love for us. There is so much about God that we just cannot comprehend, he is far above our attempts to understand him, that is why I will never think I am right and therefore other people are wrong, such thinking has missed the point of who God is.

Look for joy today.

God's all-encompassing love be with you.

Kingsley

Sat 27 June

Subject: LMA reviving

Dear Friends

In Athens Paul came across a temple to an unknown god. They had so many temples to so many gods in Athens they were afraid they might leave someone out. So when Paul spoke to them he was able to tell them who this unknown god was, he was God who unknown to them was the God who created all things, the only real God who doesn't live in temples anyway.

During this time we have found this out too, God doesn't live in the churches but he is everywhere and although we can only now go back into some churches for prayer we have all been praying all this time wherever we are. Being Christian isn't just about going to church it is how we live our lives and our witness to those around us. When more churches open and when we can begin to meet together in them for worship let us not confine ourselves to four walls but build on what we have discovered about ourselves and about God and let the church be everywhere, let it be out there among our communities. God created all things and he is still everywhere.

Every blessing

Kingsley

Sun 28 June

Subject: LMA trinity 3

Dear Friends

Matthew 10:40-end. I have never understood what pleasure people get out of being deliberately nasty or spiteful or cruel. While on the other hand today's reading tells us that there is a reward for every kindness we do for others for in doing it for others we do it for Jesus though we don't know it, and even the very act of

doing a kindness in itself is a reward. I know that there
are times you do your best to help someone and they
throw it back in your face but then that is their problem
not yours, your act of kindness will not go unnoticed by
God. After all for his act of kindness by sending his Son
led Jesus to the cross and still he was glad (if that is not
too small a word) to do it.

During this lockdown we have seen both, and perhaps
more so as things ease. Although this is nothing new
with people I suppose many of us thought that 'being in
this together' might make the world a better place. Yet
there have been so many acts of kindness and these are
not sensational enough to grab the headlines. In our
communities we see these acts of kindness at times of
bereavement anyway and it has been more widespread at
this time because there have been so many lonely and
needy people. And I know that for all the nastiness in the
world which we tend to notice because they are against
our nature there is by far a greater amount of good and
this, as I have said, does not go unnoticed by God.

Every blessing

Kingsley

Mon 29 June

Subject: LMA week 14

Dear Friends

Sitting in St Mary's for quiet prayer for an hour gave me
time to actually not pray but listen, or rather feel. There

1 is a certain brightness in the church that is at once awe
2 inspiring enough to make you feel small and comforting
3 enough to make you feel at home. I have said before
4 that there is an angel there but of course the angel
5 doesn't 'live' there, the angel is in the presence of God
6 but has a sort of presence in the church. We forget, or
7 are mostly unaware, that everywhere is in the presence
8 of God anyway and therefore so are we. The presence
9 in the church if you open up your feelings is sublime and
10 you can almost grasp the wonders of the heavenly realm
11 and are yet no overawed by it.
12
13 Having locked up I stood outside for a while. There is a
14 different spirit outside, you are still in the presence of
15 God because he is still everywhere, the presence outside
16 is more of the soil, of the grass, of the trees, of the valley
17 and you realise that God The Maker Of All Things is
18 not confined. And we are of the earth too. God has
19 given us this nature and it is not a dual nature of
20 physical and spiritual but one nature, our western
21 though tends to compartmentalise and say this is this
22 and that is that (I blame the Romans) but it is not so.
23 We are one, whole and complete and when we know
24 that we can know God as one, whole and complete and
25 still be trinity. During this time we have had to find
26 God outside the church, let us not lock him back in
27 when we can visit him on a Sunday.
28
29 Kingsley
30
31 **Tue 30 June**
32
33 Subject: LMA 100 days

Dear Friends   1
                                                          2
What is 100 days? Looking out of the study window at   3
Y Ficerdy as I tap away at the computer apart from   4
3 houses I cannot see much of Whitland although   5
I know it is there. I see hedges, trees, fields and the hills 6
the other side of the valley. This valley has been here 7
10,000 years since the last ice age. This valley has seen 8
the coming of the first settlers who were hunter gatherers 9
(there was a lake here then), then as the middle stone   10
age gave way to the new stone age they slowly became   11
farmers and erected a henge where St Mary's is as a sort 12
of calendar to mark the seasons which is important for   13
farming, it was also a place of worship and ceremonial. 14
Then as humanity grew and advanced the valley saw   15
the bronze age, the iron age, the coming of the Romans   16
and their going again, the time of the kings of Dyfed   17
down to Hywel Dda and his white house (also where   18
St Mary's is), the Cistercian monks (they also began   19
where St Mary's is before moving to where the ruined   20
abbey is now). And this is before we get to modern   21
history. So what is 100 days?   22
                                                          23
With God a day is like a thousand years (2 Pet 3:8) and 24
it is only us humans who tend to get impatient and want 25
quick answers. God will reveal what he wants us to do   26
a bit at a time as and when he is ready. In St David's 27
Archdeaconry we have two of only five churches that   28
are now open and one of those is the Cathedral and this 29
is a good first step. But I know the church has not been 30
dormant all this time as so much good has been done in   31
our communities. We do not wait, we move with God   32
and will continue to do so.   33

1 God is with you

2

3 Kingsley

4

5

Wed 1 July

6

7 Subject: LMA 2,424 hours

8

9 Dear Friends

10

11 The earth rolls on another day in the great dance of the
12 universe, the perfect balance that preserves life on this
13 ball in space. Humanity in its arrogance thinks it is all
14 powerful but it is so small and barely counts in the
15 vastness of reality. And yet God who is The Maker Of
16 All Things has a plan for our lives, we are a part of the
17 great dance, we are part of his purpose. In the eternity
18 of time our lives are but a blink and yet to him they
19 have meaning. We cannot fathom God's mind and we
20 can only glimpse the small amount he has revealed. We
21 cannot always see his purpose in our lives as it happens
22 but sometimes in looking back we can see his hand at
23 work. As I live through this life I find I have more
24 questions than answers and much as I would like to ask
25 him when I eventually see him I know when the time
26 comes I will have no questions because he is the answer.
27 Trust in him in the present moment is so hard at times,
28 he doesn't make it easy, yet we know when we do meet
29 him God himself will wipe the tears from our eyes. And
30 along the way he does give us times of joy. He has made
31 us part of his purpose and when we find his purpose for
32 us we can find fulfilment a fulfilment that those who
33 refuse to acknowledge him will for ever be looking for.

During this time I have found stillness but still feel I am no nearer understanding God.

I wish you joy this day.

Kingsley

Thu 2 July

Subject: LMA 146880 minutes

Dear Friends

There are always plusses and minuses with everything. I am on zoom any moment now, it saves traveling being able to attend meetings from home and you can't be distracted by the person sitting next to you wanting to chat, but sometimes it is nice being distracted by the person sitting next to you wanting to chat, and you have to make your own coffee and can't gather together for a chat afterwards, it is convenient but it lacks human contact as in all these technological advances. During this time it has been necessary and useful but we are all missing human contact. Even God needs human contact - if he actually needs anything that is but he does seem to yearn for it. In the Garden of Eden he used to enjoy his evening stroll and chat with Adam until Adam hid. When Jesus was on this earth he lived a normal human life, you can't tell me he didn't play with the other children, his brothers and sisters (if you are catholic ignore this last bit) and cousins, the other children of the village. During his ministry he went everywhere with his apostles, we went to wedding parties, invited himself to people's houses, he gathered people around him wherever he went.

So how does God have human contact now? Before lockdown we would go and visit him for an hour on a Sunday like an aged relative in a home, now we have to meet him everywhere we go so I hope we don't put him back in a home after. But we also meet him in one another and the kind things we do, his human contact is with us and through us. Perhaps we have had a taste of what it is like to be God unable to cwtch, unable to share a coffee and cake. Remember God when we begin to mix, he likes a chat, he likes a party, invite him in.

Kingsley

Fri 3 July

Subject: LMA 8,899,200 seconds

Dear Friends

We can go back into some of our churches to pray but we cannot sing, it looks like weddings are allowed in church but we cannot sing, in the next stage perhaps we can have some sort of service in church but we cannot sing.

The largest choir I have ever sang in was a choir of a thousand for the Billy Graham mission '89. I am a tenor and I tend to be a bit loud, or used to be, I was in Llandaff Cathedral once and I let rip and got some dirty looks from the people sitting in front. But now we

cannot sing. Because singing projects the virus such a
long way.

Since the earliest days of humanity people have sung.
There is a rhythm to life, to all life, and there is a music
to all of creation. We are a part of creation and part of
how we express ourselves is by joining in with this
rhythm and singing, sometimes on our own and sometimes with others. In England you need a good sized
church full of people so get some good singing going, in
Wales you only need a few and you have hwyl which
cannot be translated. But now we cannot sing.

Part of being in a choir is the listening so that our voices
can blend in with the others. We cannot sing but we can
listen. Listen to the music of the natural world, not just
the birds but the trees and the grass and the stars, listen
to God who creates with joy and there will be a song in
our hearts if not on our lips.

Every blessing

Kingsley

Sat 4 July

Subject: LMA tempus fugit

Dear Friends

Super Saturday in England, we have to wait a little
longer in Wales, travel restrictions will be lifted on
Monday and other things later in the week. No news of

further development with the church though, I will have to ask that since pubs and restaurants can open their gardens for food and drink soon why can't churches open their churchyards for services?

When a child first learns to walk they start by standing, then a step at a time and fall, then get up and try again and slowly get the idea of balance. As restrictions slowly ease it is like learning to walk all over again. People will be afraid of falling. But I wonder at the attitude of some people who take it so casually and crowd to beaches, the virus has not gone away. Only hindsight will tell us if we have been too cautious or too casual.

For many of us perhaps it will be like we had been walking about like caterpillars and suddenly went into a cocoon, if we emerge as butterflies then flying is going to be something new. God can change lives if we are willing to let him, do we want to fly? Butterflies can walk, they have legs, but it would be a waste of wings.

Regards

Kingsley

Sun 5 July

Subject: LMA Trinity 4

Dear Friends

The gospel reading for today is in two parts: Matt 11:16-19 where Jesus complains at the contrariness of people,

because John the Baptist doesn't eat and drink so he must
have a demon while Jesus does both and must be a
glutton and a drunkard, a friend of tax collectors and
sinners. Then 25-end where he says his message is hidden
from the wise and learned and only children can
understand it, then he promises rest for the weary.

Do we worry too much at times what other people
think of us, surely it is best to be true to ourselves.
There is too much pressure to conform and little scope
for individuality. I have tried to be myself in these
emails and even I will admit I can be a bit strange at
times. However I was thanked recently for not talking
down to you, well how can I when I am not a wise and
learned super being who can quote scripture and verse
and expound on it in great detail. I cannot preach to
save my life because I am no better than anyone else, we
are all pilgrims on a journey through life trying to
understand the world, ourselves and God and don't
seem to be getting any closer to an understanding.

But todays lesson has the answer, we shouldn't try to
understand, just accept that God is with us on our
journey and enjoy the sights as we go along and he will
give us rest for our souls.

Peace be with you

Kingsley

Mon 6 July

Subject: LMA week 15

Dear Friends

The past is unchangeable but history is another thing. The Bible deals with historical events but is not a history, it is the Jewish people and the early church trying to understand God and their relationship to him, the Romans didn't write history rather they wrote propaganda, the Celts didn't write but a lot of their history is legend. When I did my dissertation for my MA that became the history of the Whitland group of Parishes from the end of the Roman occupation until the Middle Ages and until someone disagrees that is the true history, except I know there is an error in it which no one has pointed out to me. History changes with who wrote it and why.

Take the four Gospels, Mark and Luke were not direct witnesses of Jesus ministry but Matthew and John were and their memories of Jesus were different and this makes it all the more true because eye witness accounts will never be the same while a false account will be the same agreed story.

We are living through a historical event, each of us will have different memories of what it was like, people in towns and cities will have different memories again, historians of the future looking back will put their own interpretation on things.

As Pilate asked Jesus, 'what is truth?' Jesus didn't answer because Pilate immediately walked away. Jesus often used the phrase 'I tell you the truth ...' if he had something important to tell the disciples, for he is the way and the truth and the life. In a world of opinions and shifting ideas it is good to know there is some solid ground.

Regards

Kingsley

Tue 7 July

Subject: LMA Another day

Dear Friends

Yesterday in Wales we could travel wherever we wanted, so where can we go? What do we do with our new freedom? Those with grandchildren can go and visit and cuddle them so I expect there was a lot of that going on. No one in Wales died of Covid 19 yesterday, but this is not the only health issue and the virus is still around. You can get married in church with limits but no ordinary services allowed only prayer.

Coming slowly out of lockdown is another strange time, knowing what we can do and what we can't, feeling confident enough with what we can do. We are constantly learning through this. Although I have zoomed I cannot organise a zoom meeting properly myself, I was born B.C. (before computers) and technology is still very much an enigma. And until I can pop in to see someone I will feel like a fish out of water.

Still each new day brings something new and things are beginning to move. I wonder what today will bring.

Kingsley

Wed 8 July

Subject: LMA And another day

Dear Friends

It is good to know that the number of deaths are settling down to normal for this time of year, but this is a statistic and it still means that people are dying with all the heartache and loss that their families have to face. I hope we haven't become cold to the sadness there is in the world. But this is life and nature. There are births and celebrations of anniversaries and weddings can take place again. So let us not lose sight of joy either.

Although we are slowly emerging we face a different world, a new way of doing things. No news yet about services in church or in the open air and I look forward to that. But at what point do these emails stop? Maybe not at all but not so regular?

I am still reflecting, twice a week in Church now, and there is still the possibility of some blinding revelation from God. In the meantime the still small voice is there and there is activity in the heavenly realms. There is more joy to come.

Keep faith

Kingsley

Thu 9 July

Subject: LMA New day

Dear Friends

There are times I feel like I have somehow emigrated to another country where, although many things are familiar and they still speak the same language, they have different customs and I'm not sure what they are. Or I have slipped through to a parallel universe where it is the similar but different.

How much we took for granted before and it was easy to just drift through life doing the same things we always did, now even simple things we have to think about and assess the risks especially as the lockdown eases though the virus hasn't gone away.

I can't help thinking about the early disciples, fishermen, tax collectors, leather workers, tent makers and so forth, now they have had to leave the familiar behind as they go out into the world taking Jesus' message.

But every day is a new day, it is not a repeat of yesterday or last week, and we should appreciate each new day for the promise it holds.

Enjoy today

Kingsley

Fri 10 July

Subject: LMA New dawn

Dear Friends

If we look back over our lives is there a point where we were happiest, is there a time that we wish we could go back to? The danger is that we hang on to this and don't appreciate what we have now. Especially if now is a dark and sad time (and before you ask this is not where I am). But tomorrow, the future? If we dwell in the past we will miss the possibility of tomorrow. In fact the future starts now and most of today (unless you read this last thing at night) is still future and there are possibilities and surprises.

God has the advantage of being outside time and can look at our past and our future as one thing, but we are bound in time so our best chance is to trust him.

I feel this present situation is worse for children for this should be a carefree time for them and I do wonder what memories they will have to look back on. So we who are adults should not grumble.

As for me, I am an annoying optimist, now is always the best time for me and the future is always going to be better.

Be surprised today

Kingsley

Sat 11 July

Subject: LMA New hope

Dear Friends

The disciples had seen miracles surrounding Jesus which
gave weight to the things he said but the message was
always more important so he would withdraw when
people followed him for the wrong reason. Because
they had seen miracles they had the simple faith to
know they happened so miracles would follow them as
well but again it was the message that was important,
the miracles only added weight to their words.

The Celtic Church saw miracles too because of their
simple faith that miracles were a natural part of life.

So it is one of those difficulties we have now, why don't
we see miracles? Do we not have the simple faith? Has
life become too complicated? Have we separated what
is physical and what is spiritual? Or do we see miracles
all the time and take them for granted? After all we do
not need to put on a show to perform miracles (and
I hate the word perform when attached to miracles),
they should follow naturally in ordinary situations.

Each new day, the growing things all around us, the
birth of a new life, God's world is full of wonders. Once
we can see miracles everywhere perhaps our simple faith
will also see the special miracles.

Believe

Kingsley

Sun 12 July

Subject: LMA Trinity V

1 Dear Friends

2

3 Today's gospel is the parable of the sower, the sower
4 throws his seed everywhere and it depends on the
5 ground whether the seed even sinks in, or shoots up
6 only to wither away, or gets strangled with weeds, or
7 produces a rich crop. This, as Jesus explains to his
8 disciples, is a picture of God giving his good news and
9 his promises to everyone, it is up to everyone how this
10 is received. There are those whose hearts are so hard
11 they don't even receive it, the shallow people who
12 believe only for a moment, those who get so entangled
13 with other things they have no room for good news,
14 and those who truly accept what God has given and
15 are so full of joy they affect everyone they come in
16 contact with.

17

18 The lockdown has given us all a chance to reflect but it
19 has changed no one's nature though it may have
20 highlighted the sort of person we are, whether hard and
21 selfish or kind and giving.

22

23 If we go back to the parable the one thing that has
24 always stood out with me is that if the sower is sowing
25 the seed indiscriminately then it is still in a field and
26 although there are beaten paths, rocks and weeds it is
27 still a field and therefore most of the soil is good. There
28 are so many more good people in this world than bad, it
29 is just that we notice the bad more because they stick
30 out and in the greater world they are the ones who get
31 into the news, if only the news would report more on
32 people like Captain Tom Moore, the doctors, nurses
33 and key workers etc.

Be good

Kingsley

Mon 13 July

Subject: LMA week 16

Dear Friends

When I started this it was not straight away when the lockdown began but a couple of days later and it was just to let everyone I had an email for in the LMA know that although the church buildings had suddenly shut the church was still here. Then another one a few days later just to keep in touch. It was only because of Holy Week that I thought it would be a good idea to do a daily reflection up until Easter, it was only the response from those of you who were receiving it that it became a regular daily email, and since then it has grown, every week someone else wants to be added to the list and it is no longer just the LMA, I send it all over the country and even abroad.

Why this long rambling explanation? Simply this, we can't always hear what God is saying in an obvious way but as long as we do our little best to do some good he will take our effort and with the help of others make something of it. I can't help thinking of the picture on the fridge. Your children or grandchildren paint a picture, it is not a Renoir or Constable but you are so proud of it you put it on your fridge (or wherever) for

everyone to see. We are God's children, don't think the
picture has to be perfect just give it to him.

Paint away

Kingsley

Part 9 Amber Phase

Tue 14 July

Subject: LMA budding

Dear Friends

First I need the permission of the LMA to apply to hold
services in St Mary's and a separate application for an
open air service at St Mary's, if I don't hear any dissen-
tions I will take it as permission. Any other churches
wishing to open for services look up

https://www.churchinwales.org.uk/en/clergy-and-
members/coronavirus-covid-19-guidance/re-opening-
churches/

then get back to me and I will ask permission of the
LMA for you.

The world is a wonderful place, it is the people in it that
are so strange. Some people are so casual and think
nothing of crowding together while others are now too
frightened to go out at all, everyone is an individual and
when dealing with people you must accept them where
they are. One size doesn't fit all. Listening is far more
important than telling.

The first service I would like to take at St Mary's is the
open air one for the whole LMA I promised and I do
not want to do all the talking. Bearing in mind social

1 distancing it would be nice if individuals would be
2 willing to come to wherever we decide the front is to
3 pray, reflect, share but I would like to know beforehand
4 who would be willing to do this so we can do it in an
5 orderly way. If you read the guidelines we can only do
6 this on church grounds which means the churchyard so
7 we have to be respectful of the graves, think about this
8 and come back to me. And by the way, if you need a
9 chair please bring your own.

10

11 Apologies if you were expecting my usual rambling
12 thoughts today.

13

14 Kingsley

15

16
Wed 15 July
17

18 Subject: LMA sprouting

19

20 Dear Friends

21

22 I have an admission to make. As the lockdown eases I
23 have mixed emotions. I feel that at the beginning of the
24 lockdown things were so simple, we knew where we
25 were hard though it was, the sun was shining and it
26 seemed nature was taking a rest and I did hope people
27 were having to reassess everything, and yet I feel guilty
28 for thinking this way because people were suffering and
29 dying and worried about their futures and many were
30 lonely and isolated.

31

32 Now as things open up it seems as if the world is
33 crowding back in again.

Yet I am excited too, having opened some churches for prayer we can now think about simple services, I have even been asked about a wedding.

What complicated beings we are! I don't even understand myself so how can I possibly understand anyone else let alone judge them?

Yours confused

Kingsley

Thu 16 July

Subject: LMA flowering

Dear Friends

I think it was a warning that Bilbo gave to Frodo in the Lord of the Rings about being careful when stepping onto the road through the Shire because you never know where it will take you. It had taken Bilbo to the desolation of Smaug but it had brought him back with great wealth. It took Frodo to Mount Doom and although it won him great fame he was never the same when he came back and he couldn't stay in Middle Earth.

We were forced onto this road back in March and for a while we coped but from your responses yesterday I am not the only one finding the road harder. Yet travel this road we must because there is no going back, there are adventures to come, difficulties to overcome and new people to meet along the way and old friends to catch up with.

However the whole of life is a journey and this pandemic has woken us up out of our drift through life to think more about what we are doing and where we are going. All of a sudden nothing was certain, this is ok for people who like a challenge but we must be aware of the needs and concerns of others around us on the journey who do not cope so well with uncertainty. Always remember we are not alone on this journey, we have each other and we have Jesus as our guide.

Step boldly into the future

Kingsley

Fri 17 July

Subject: LMA blossoming

Dear Friends

I have been asked how I manage with this email every day, has it become a chore, what do I find to say all the time? The answer is all of you. I have had such encouraging replies, times when it has really helped someone, this email is a two way street and I appreciate all those who find time to reply. As I said this is not a journey we are taking alone we are together. It must be hard for people who do travel alone for one reason or another.

Many years ago pilgrims would travel to St David's 1
Cathedral, it was easier than going to Jerusalem and 3 2
visits to St David's was equivalent to going to Jerusalem, 3
and Whitland was one of the stop over places on 4
the way. The important people (!) would go to the 5
Cistercian Abbey for the night (though there was a 6
complaint that the hospitality was so good they never 7
got any further), while everyone else would camp out in 8
the chapel of ease where St Mary's is now. On the 9
surface of it the so called important people had a better 10
time but I am sure everyone else actually did, there is a 11
joy in sharing when people travel together and rough it 12
together because we can be ourselves and not have to 13
put on a show. I am sure the church did much better 14
when times were harder, when there weren't all these 15
impressive basilicas and high ranking clerics in costly 16
robes. We in our parishes among the people is where 17
the church is. 18
19
Kingsley 20
21
22
Sat 18 July
23
Subject: LMA fruiting 24
25
Dear Friends 26
27
Suddenly I am very busy again, next week my diary is 28
full already. Quite apart from all these risk assessment 29
forms I have to fill in just to get things going in church. 30
Weather permitting the open air LMA gathering service 31
in St Mary's Churchyard is arranged for Sunday 2nd 32
Aug at 11.00 am, I have to fill in a risk assessment form 33

for that and get it passed by the Archdeacon. For the
risk assessment I need to know who wishes to speak in
advance, so if you would like to pray, read, reflect or
whatever (NO PREACHING) so you can stand in your
6ft protective zone close enough to the front so you can
step up to the microphone (after it is wiped) without
passing too many people.

Oh what strange times we live in, all the time we are
having to think of what we are doing, whether going
to the shop, seeing family, going to work, the list is
endless. But I hope we are still finding time to look
around and see the wonders of God's creation and
greet people on the road (6ft away). It is a strange fact
of life that there is always sadness and joy next to each
other the virus has only made us more aware of this.
There are times I am sure that we are dreaming all this
and we will wake to find none of it happened, but
mostly it seems like we had been dreaming all along
and now we are awake and aware of more and appreciate more of what we have. I hope also that we
have drawn closer to one another (6ft away) and to
God (no social distancing there).

God be with you.

Kingsley

Sun 19 July

Subject: LMA Trinity 6

Dear Friends

Gen 28:10-19a the Old Testament reading for today. 1
Jacob was a crafty so and so, he had pinched Esau's 2
blessing from their father by wearing his clothes and 3
putting goatskin on his neck and now he was on the run 4
from Esau. Now as the sun set he was a long way from 5
anywhere so he took a stone for his pillow and lay 6
down to sleep where he was. In the night he had a 7
vision of a ladder reaching up into heaven with angels 8
going up and down. In the morning he realised that he 9
had been on holy ground so set up the stone and called 10
the place Bethel. 11
12
During lockdown with the churches closed I hope we 13
have all found holy ground where we least expected it. 14
We have been closer to God all the time without realis- 15
ing it. It is good to have a place to gather for communal 16
worship but God, the Maker Of All Things is every- 17
where and not just limited to certain places. The Celts 18
recognised though that there were places where God 19
seem to be closer than others and these they called 'Thin 20
Places' not that he was closer but rather that we feel 21
closer to him. 22
23
St Non's is a special place for me, I had gone through 24
my three years training in St Michael's college and 25
preparing for Ordination in St David's Cathedral, all of 26
us who were preparing were on retreat at St. Non's 27
retreat house. In those days two people shared a room 28
and the chap I shared with was a fitness fan and he 29
would get up early in the morning and go for a run. 30
Unable to sleep I got up too but went and sat on the 31
clifftop to talk to God. Was I really sure this is what 32
I wanted to do? Could I lead others in a spiritual 33

journey? Could I be a Vicar of a church (or churches)?
I wasn't sure I could. After several days I eventually I
said to God "No, I can't do this unless you help me."
and God said "Good." The only clear word I have ever
had from him, but at least I met God in a special way on
the cliff top near St Non's.

Meet with God today

Kingsley

Mon 20 July

Subject: LMA Week 17

Dear Friends

I was outside the paper shop in Whitland the other day
talking to a woman I know by sight but not her name.
She said that she had been in self-isolation and when she
decided it was time to actually come out to the shops it
took her a whole two weeks to summon up the courage
to do so, not because of the virus she assured me but she
was afraid to leave her home because she had been shut
in so long.

Who has not felt 'pushed' from behind simply because
the person behind you in a queue or in a shop is closer
than six feet?

We have the double fear of the virus and the easing of
the lockdown.

Yesterday in St Mary's I had Taize music playing quietly
in the background and I don't always pay attention to
the words, but the chant that begins 'In the Lord ...' has
the line 'do not be afraid.'

Kingsley

Tue 21 July

Subject: LMA quiet

Dear Friends

One of the greatest gifts God gave us was our human
heart with all its problems and if we are made in his
image then our heart is an image of his and perhaps it is
there that we can understand him best if we are willing to
do so. Our hearts can be fickle at times, they can lead us
into bad decisions but it is there we appreciate what we
have the most, the world in all its beauty our friends and
loved ones. It is there we feel sadness and hurt, it is there
we feel compassion, it is there we can know joy.

Can a person crush their own heart, make it hard as
rock, ignore it? Can a person let bitterness, greed, hate
eat away at it so it becomes dark? And after all that can
it live again? God can take a heart of stone and make it
flesh again but he will not do so unless asked, but a
heart is never entirely dead and only he knows the way
through to it.

But those who listen to their heart, those willing to feel
sadness and joy, to experience the welling up of deep

1 emotion even if we don't know where this has come
2 from it can be a rollercoaster. Better that than a drab,
3 monotonous existence.
4
5 Kingsley
6
7
8 **Wed 22 July**
9 Subject: LMA peace
10
11 Dear Friends
12
13 I'm sure we have done a lot of reflection over these past
14 months, and there is more than one meaning to this.
15 The dictionary givers a technical meaning about light,
16 heat or sound thrown back off a surface but when you
17 see the moon reflected in the surface of a still lake it is
18 far more romantic and it will lead to the reflection in
19 your own being of what it means to you to see the moon
20 reflected. Or when you look at yourself in a mirror
21 what do you see? Do you reflect on who that person is?
22 And there is a third meaning that is to do with the con-
23 sequences of past actions or a way of life. Reflection is
24 a word with such depths. Reflections can be confusing
25 when you see something reflected in a window by
26 chance without realising it is a reflection and you can't
27 make it out because it is in the wrong place and the
28 wrong way round or in the night you see a light that can
29 be a reflection of a reflection from two different
30 windows and you can't make it out.
31
32 We can only see God in a reflection dimly (1 Cor 13)
33 now so how can anyone claim to know God better than

anyone else? Yet God is the reality behind the reflection
and though we only glimpse him he knows us perfectly.

Every blessing

Kingsley

Thu 23 July

Subject: LMA silence

Dear Friends

In case you hadn't heard or seen it there is a bright
comet in the sky, Neowise. If you look for the plough
then come down slightly to the right and half way to the
horizon there it is. Impressive? Not really, it is a fuzzy
patch that it takes a while to spot, but at least you can
see it with the naked eye (on a clear night anyway).
I was looking for something spectacular.

Comets are supposed to herald some catastrophe aren't
they, some portent of doom? In which case why wasn't
it obvious just before the pandemic, why now as things
are easing? This is probably because it is a large piece
of rock and ice in space that has come close enough
to the sun for the solar radiation to melt it and throw a
'tail' off it. But people like to see significance in unusual
events in the sky. Yet we are bound to the natural world
as well as the spiritual, our bodies are made up of the
same atoms as the stars, as Delenne in Babylon 5 says
we are the universe trying to make sense of itself. We
are the very matter that makes everything and we have

intelligence to try and understand and we have the likeness of God in us to see beyond and believe there is more.

Perhaps we can see significance in thing because sometimes there is, not necessarily comets. For whatever reason the pandemic happened it did give us space to reflect, to examine ourselves and our relationship with God, but how many people have done that and how many have wasted the opportunity.

Every blessing

Kingsley

Fri 24 July

Subject: LMA rest

Dear Friends

Early on in these emails I hinted at my very strange belief system. I also said I had a fundamentalist beginning but that experience had mellowed that. I'm sure you have all worked out by now that although I did my training in St Michael's Theological College which is tractarian I am by no means high church. However I do hold on to some high church principles. I am also very definitely not liberal, the truth doesn't change with current fashion. Nor am I charismatic or Pentecostal. I am not exactly low church either. So here is the riddle then, where do I fit in among the wide range of Anglican labels?

The answer is that I hate labels and refuse to stay in a
pigeon hole. I had to fill in a form a year or two ago for
the diocese and on it I had to put what my churchmanship
was so I called myself a mystic. I hate labels so much
I will not label anyone else I will not even answer the
question 'how old was he?' Everyone is an individual,
everyone is special, everyone is unique. This is part of
the reason I still put all your emails in individually
rather than try to find out how to do it as a block, so
I can think of you all as individuals as I do it. I think of
the replies I have had and who responds to what sort of
message. I wonder at the choice of email addresses that
you have, and in case you are wondering at ktaylor559
I tried all sorts but Aol kept suggesting ktaylor559 so
I got stuck with it. We all have our stories and our
experiences and one of the best things you can do for
anyone is to listen and value what they say. Everyone's
opinion or point of view is valid, even when we don't
agree. Glory in our differences.

Kingsley

Sat 25 July

Subject: Stillness

Dear Friends

We tend to fill our lives with things, we almost feel
guilty when we are not doing anything, and those who
are happy with not doing anything fill the space with
other things like television and computer games. One
way or another so many people shun stillness and quiet.

The foundation of Cyffig church is a monastic cell that dates back at least to Viking times because of the name, but it is likely that it is from much earlier times. It was a place where a hermit lived for the solitude, for the quiet, for the opportunity to know himself and God better. This isn't to say he was always on his own, he would have been part of a group of such people scattered around who did get together from time to time and local people would have come to see him bringing him supplies and seeking his wisdom. And this is so far removed from the church that has to have zoom meetings to show it is still active, some I am sure are necessary but all of them?

Not all people are meant to be hermits and some have found the isolation difficult, we are not all the same. As I get busier I feel more prepared because I did find some space to be quiet and reflect, up until the lockdown I was rushing around far too much that I was feeling unwell and didn't know why. In my last zoom meeting I was told I ought to have a holiday, but living where I do is like being on holiday all the time and a holiday would be filling my time with something else. Besides, I couldn't do this on holiday.

Kingsley

Sun 26 July

Subject: LMA Trinity 7

Dear Friends

Matthew 13 31-33, 44-52. The kingdom of heaven is 1
like a mustard seed, yeast mixed in with a large amount 2
of flour, treasure hidden in a field, a pearl of great price, 3
a net let down into a lake. Taking the mustard seen and 4
the yeast the kingdom of heaven is all around us, 5
running through everything, we are always close to the 6
kingdom of heaven and can shelter there already. Yet 7
taking the treasure and the pearl it is not easy to find 8
even when it is right under our nose and it is of such 9
great value there is nothing to compare. And the net in 10
the lake tells us there is judgement to come, all are 11
gathered in but the good and the bad are separated. 12
13
Jesus gave us stories to illustrate the truth rather than 14
theological explanations or lectures, he shows us mean- 15
ing in every day events. The truth is all around us in 16
everything God has made so you don't need a sermon 17
from me. Find the kingdom of heaven everywhere you 18
go today and in everything you do. 19
20
God is with you 21
22
Kingsley 23
24
25
Mon 27 July
26
Subject: LMA week 18 27
28
Dear Friends 29
30
Yesterday I was reading and praying and reflecting in 31
St Mary's and I had to admit to myself about something 32
that has been rankling with me not since the beginning 33

of the lockdown but from very early on. I was reminded
of something very profound so I let go of my concern.

What is the difference between clergy and laity?
Absolutely nothing, except clergy tend to think they are
special. Who is the church? You are. After all through
all these months where have I had the support? From
Jo-an and from you. Your responses have been very
moving at times and I am honoured that you have
shared so much with me. We draw strength from each
other, we support each other, we care for each other.
This is what Jesus came to show us as he travelled
around with his friends, read the gospels and see where
he had support and where he had opposition. In every
aspect of life it is not the leaders or the politicians who
run the world it is everyone who just get on with it
without having to hold meetings.

Thank you for everything

Kingsley

Tue 28 July

Subject: LMA Mystery

Dear Friends

In a world where you can find an answer to almost
everything on Google is there anything left we cannot
know? We can take a virtual trip around the world as
many people have during lockdown is there anywhere
left we cannot see? If you go on to Google Earth and

zoom in to the Vicarage here you can see the new 1
Ficerdy being built but when you go on to street view 2
the roman road is as it was with a bank and trees and 3
no sign of Y Ficerdy. The internet is only as good as the 4
last time it was updated and the information on it only 5
as good as what has been put in by someone. You can 6
find people explaining all sorts of mysteries on Youtube 7
but have salt with you so you can pinch it. The internet 8
is a tool and cannot replace real life. 9

10

As lockdown eases it is time to let go of technology, get 11
out and experience the world again strange as it is. 12
Meet up with people again from a safe distance. As 13
long as the weather is good enough on Sunday you are 14
all invited to the open air service at St Mary's at 11.00 15
am, though Bedfordshire, Herefordshire, Snowdonia, 16
Bristol, France and Canada (and wherever else some of 17
you are) are a bit far to come just for that. We all need 18
to live again as I am sure the lockdown has affected 19
everyone and some worse than others. It is not over and 20
will not be for a long time but all of life is a risk and we 21
need to live and experience the real world. 22

23

24

Enjoy today 25

26

Kingsley 27

28

29

Wed 29 July

30

Subject: LMA puzzle 31

32

Dear Friends 33

Both Jo-an and I have needed an actual bank for some time and yesterday we got up the courage to go to Carmarthen. While there we went to a couple of shops too. You will never believe how nervous I was! We used to go to Carmarthen once a fortnight and thought nothing of it. Coming out of lockdown into this foreign world is slow and complicated. Some of you may think I am strange because you are finding it easier.

We all go at our own pace. When living our Christian lives and spreading the good news we cannot all be evangelists, some are apostles, some prophets, some pastors and teachers, each of us has a role to play which God has for us, he knows us and our capabilities better than we do ourselves. When he asks us to do something we are not sure of it is because he trusts us and knows we are able to do it even when we don't.

Let God take you by the hand and lead you

Kingsley

Thu 30 July

Subject: LMA Enigma

Dear Friends

Have you ever thought what a wonderful being you are? You only have to watch the development of a baby to realise how many things each of us had to learn very quickly, to learn to recognise faces and expressions, to learn language and communication, to learn

coordination and balance, to understand symbols as 1
letters and collections of letters as words, to be able to 2
use the variety of tools and gadgets, the list goes on. 3
And through all this you have an imagination and the 4
ability to understand beyond what it obvious. You are 5
self-aware and aware also that there are other things 6
beyond so that you can reach out to the infinite, the 7
divine, and know God. You can learn from the past in 8
order to live in the present and face with confidence the 9
future. You can forge friendships and communities so 10
you are never alone. You have the full range of feelings 11
and emotions, not all of which you can understand. 12
13
So what is the greatest of all the things you are? Your 14
capacity to love, the least understood and yet the most 15
powerful. Do not stifle it with hate or bitterness or envy 16
or greed. 17
18
Do not waste anything that you are by shutting it off or 19
filling your life with things that do not matter. Be the 20
complete wonderful person you are, the person God 21
made you to be. 22
23
Kingsley 24
25
26
Fri 31 July
27
Subject: LMA conundrum 28
29
Dear Friends 30
31
When I was taught about bereavement counselling the 32
three worst events in someone's life was the loss of a 33

loved one, divorce and moving home. I wonder where pandemic comes into this? Of course we are all grieving, everyone has lost many things including a way of life, we must be prepared for the feelings that go with grief. To face this and accept it is part of the process and each of us will deal with it differently. Normally I could call round but even that is denied. Now more than ever we need each other.

But as I said yesterday we are all wonderful beings, we have a tremendous capacity for joy and hope, we will make the best of this and we will be stronger as a result. If a second wave comes we will deal with that too.

In the future when this is mostly behind us we will be able to say when anything happens, "What is the worst that can happen? It can't be worse than the pandemic we will cope with this too."

1 Cor 16:13 Be on your guard; stand firm in the faith; be people of courage; be strong. Do everything in love.

Kingsley

Sat 1 Aug

Subject: LMA riddle

Dear Friends

I was rubbish at history when I was in school, I was not interested in the kings of England and I can't even remember what else we were supposed to be interested

in. So isn't it strange that I am so interested in history
now, probably because it is history of my choosing,
the history of where I live and the job I am doing. Also
it is because it gives us perspective. For when we live
through difficult times we know there are always good
times, happy times, to follow. And one day this will be
history too.

The cycle of the world shows us that in the depths of
winter, the dark, wet and cold days, spring will always
follow, and even if summer is wet and miserable a fine
settled autumn will follow. In the dark hours of the
night, around 2 and 3, the hour of the wolf, when we
cannot sleep for cares and worries the sun will rise
eventually and we have faced each new day before and
will face this next one too. When it rains and suddenly
the sun comes out there is a rainbow which is God's
promise to the world.

Genesis 8:22 As long as the earth endures, seedtime and
harvest, cold and heat, summer and winter, day and
night will never cease.

We are collectively going through a hard time now but
there is such joy and happiness ahead and we will see it.

God bless you all

Kingsley

Part 10 The End?

Sun 2 Aug

Subject: LMA trinity 8

Dear Friends

Matthew 14:13-21. John the Baptist has just been beheaded and when Jesus heard he just wanted to get away, they were cousins and he needed to mourn. But he had no chance, crowds followed and Jesus had compassion on them, their needs came before his own, he healed the sick, he taught them, then he fed them because it was late and the place was remote. This is the context of the feeding of the five thousand, sometimes we forget Jesus had feelings too. And isn't it often the case that those who need help themselves are the ones others put demands on, because those who suffer themselves are the very ones who show more compassion to others.

And yet, those who need help themselves rather than shut themselves away gain so much more in the very act of helping others. This has been a time when everyone has suffered and so much caring for one another in our communities has been the shining highlight of it all. In this mixed up world there is so much more good than bad, it just doesn't make headlines. There is so much love and compassion in the world still that far outweighs the hatred and spite, look for the good in people today.

Go in peace to love and serve

Kingsley

Mon 3 Aug

Subject: LMA week 19

Dear Friends

Thank you all who attended the open air service yesterday. I felt we had reached an important milestone. From now on there will be simple services inside St Mary's every Sunday at 11.00. Still no singing. If this was a story this would be a good place to finish and I would no longer send my daily emails. But this is not a story and it is not the end.

Ever since the lake that filled the valley after the last ice age broke through and flooded away the site where we were has been an important place to gather and to give thanks to a power greater than ourselves. The Neolithic people made it what we now term as a henge after stone henge though obviously on a smaller scale and the stones they brought down from Preseli and placed there at some point were taken away to add to the stones at stone henge. To call them pagan is to attach all sorts of bad preconceptions to them. They were simply trying to make sense of a world they didn't understand and powers greater than them that with the fuller revelation of God through Jesus we understand somewhat better. Sometime between 10,000 and 6,000 years ago until now it has been an important place for people to gather together for worship. In a way, yesterday was a thanksgiving because now we can gather again.

I have got used to being brief but the way people were hanging about yesterday I don't suppose any one would

have minded if I had been a bit long winded. But I don't
suppose I could preach again like I used to, nor would
I feel comfortable in a pulpit. These emails have been
very personal at times and I don't want to set myself
apart.

Every blessing

Kingsley

Lightning Source UK Ltd.
Milton Keynes UK
UKHW011137111220
374926UK00001B/70

9 781839 752971